Oops! Pops

By Raymond (Ray) Leslie Bigsby

Published: 11/2013

Dedicated to my family and friends

Prologue

I must confess that I don't recall a whole lot about my preschool years. I am sure that I was born in the county of Genasee. Our home place was Clio, a small town north of Flint. Actually, it was two miles south of Clio at a small area where Bingham school was located. This is where Bingham road went left off Clio road. If I recall right, it may have been a half a mile or perhaps a full mile down Bingham road to where Jameson Drive went to the left, the house in which we lived in during this period was located on the corner of Bingham and Jameson Drive. 2266 Jameson Drive was the place.

Bingham road was not a very long road, unless a person were to continue beyond the school to the West, but I don't think that it did, then if you go East on Bingham you will cross the railroad tracks, then if you go a short distance after you cross over the tracks you will come to a small one lane dirt trail that will cut a cross Bingham causing it to come to a dead end. Now, while you are traveling down Bingham road, to the East, you will come to a small hill to an important landmark in the life and times of yours truly, you will approach a bridge, once you have crossed the bridge and gone up the other side of the hill you will come to a dirt road going to the left (North) this dirt road is named Jameson Drive. I am not really sure about this next fact but I do believe that the property on the west side of Jameson drive had belonged to my grandfather [pa Jameson]. Grandpa {John}, was married to grandma (Frances), they lived in a rather small house across the wash from where we lived.

There is no way that I could put a year on it but Pa and Ma Jameson moved to Oceana County on the bank of the Pentwater River. (Remember this river will come back in play several times in the future.) It was here that they, Pa and Ma, I assume bought an old farm house with several acres of farm land. On this farm, Pa and grandma staid for most of their life, perhaps with a short wile they stayed in the Fourthward of Ludington. There will be more about the farm later.

The house that we lived in was a small house. The house was not in very good shape. However, this is what we called home for the Bigsby bunch. This included, our father, Clyde our mother, Gladys, the siblings consisted of the oldest Leon, then came Milbert, then Leroy, Harry ,Ray, Bob, Duane. This included all of the brothers, but we sure would not want to leave out our sister

Betty or the youngest of them all Barbara. Oh, my, there was a boy named Darrell, Darrell died shortly after birth, he would have been the oldest of the ten of the Bigsby bunch.

Starting on back: left to right: Leon, Leroy, Milbert, Clyde Sylvester Bigsby (dad) Front, Bob, Me, Duane

Starting on back left to right: Leroy, Ray, Leon, Bob, Milbert

Front row: Mary (Leroy's wife) Barbara and Betty

Chapter One

Now is the time for me to really get things confused. The reason I say that is, I for one am confident that some of the things that I refer to are not necessarily in the order in which they occurred. However, if you can dispute these facts then I may agree with you, that you are perhaps much more accurate than I am, but I probably won't change the things I recall because this is about what I remember. With that said, let us continue. I will go on with a group of stories that pop into my head.

Here are a few incidents that occurred during my very young age. I recall a neighbor, E.T. LaValley was preparing some scrap metal for the market, and like most small kids, this was something new and exciting, so like all two to three year olds I jumped at the chance to help this nice fellow. So I pulled on a pair of rubber boots. (Now you may need to know that this was probably in the summer or perhaps early fall.) The reason I say that is because it was very unusual for the Bigsby bunch to wear shoes at this time of year.

Now the boots may have belonged to Mr. LaValley so obviously they were much too large for this little boy's foot. Since I now had on some big boy work boots I must have been feeling my grown up manly hood. Most people that knew me realized that I was very clumsy so they no doubt understood how this could have happened, when I stepped up to the line to pick up that five hundred pound, (or perhaps in my mind I may have imagined it to have weighed a lot, but it may have been just a very few pounds. I may need to share some important facts with you.)

First of all, do you recall when I referred to Grand pa Jameson living across the <u>wash</u>? Well this is sometimes referred to by some folks as a gully, caused by water from either rain or perhaps melting snow in the spring. It is not unusual for people to put rocks in a wash to slow the washing effect of the water. When water rushes through a culvert it corrodes the soil and makes even a deeper gully, this is called erosion. This gully is the same one that I referred to a moment ago when I said Pa Jameson lived just across the wash.

With this in mind, I boldly pick up my heavy load and commenced to carry my heavy load to a point where we were to pile the iron pieces. However, with those boots, my clumsiness, and the rocks that I had to travel over or around, I might have reached my destination. I was doing real well until somehow I tripped. My right index finger ended up between the piece of iron and one of those rocks and a small cut into my finger was noticeable. I am sure that this cut, according to the scar left on my finger today was very serious. You know even with the cut, the severed tendon, torn ligament, and broken bone, guess it was not that bad.

I suppose you wonder how that I can say such a thing. I will explain. If a person were to sustain an injury of this magnitude even if it were an adult it would at least cause them to want to cry. Well, even at my age, maybe three years old, I do not recall whimpering nor crying a bit, (There you go again your mind is telling you that this cannot be possible.) However, I may agree that this may not be right but I remind you that I don't recall crying, it sure is great to get older and you can no longer remember some of the more unpleasant things.

Not too long after the episode with the finger, I recall a very serious accident that seemed to follow along side me wherever I was to go. First of all, it may be interesting for my readers too know that the Bigsby bunch had a lean to shack that we called a barn. This barn was located between the house and the creek that meandered along the full length of our property.

Mentioning this creek has reminded me of something that had happened along the creek so doesn't let me forget to come back to it.

Now back to the horse, oh I am sorry I forgot to mention the horse or did I? Well, you can see how my memory is not my best suit. You think about it, it would be useless to have a barn without some sort of animal to put in it. In our case our animal was a horse or was it a mule or perhaps it may have been a donkey. As you can tell I just don't remember what it was; however, that is not so important how it got done as to what I am trying to get across. It is very clear in my mind that this incident occurred probably during the summer days. Again, as it was a custom I was not wearing shoes. Well, if you can just picture a group of excited unruly kids crowding around this, let's call it a Shetland pony, all of them are I imagine scurrying around trying to get the older kids to let them have a ride. Then all of a sudden, the pony's horse shoe clad hoof was on top of my little bare foot. My foot was no match for this unsuspecting animal. It was awful, I can remember my mother picking me up in to her arms and taking me to the house. Again, I do not recollect any tears or pain .I cannot imagine with the severity of this injury that I must have wailed for a long, long time. According to the scar on my foot it must have nearly taken four toes off my foot. It appears to me that it must have taken quite a while to put this little guys foot back together again. Now it is time to move on to another experience in our story.

Do you recall in the last story that I had asked you to remind me of the creek? Well, this may take a spell. Let me give you a run down on a few things that I remember about this body of water that passed through our land. I am not real sure about this, if I recall however, I am not real sure a about a lot of things that I have related to!

I am not sure where the creek gets its start from but it may originate from a small lake located just to the east of the railroad tracks, once you leave the lake the creek approaches and goes under the railroad tracks. Now they have constructed a trestle to allow the water to pass through without the water causing damage to the tracks. Now I will tell you this the water after a heavy rain or in the spring when the snow melts in the spring there is an abundance of water causing the creek to rise until it occasionally floods its banks. It just dawned on me, after one of those big rains we were playing in the creek when we noticed that the water was much darker then usual. In this dark water several fish swimming along with their mouths out of the water I assume trying to get air that was not in the water because it was so murky. At least it looked much worse then it usually did. Perhaps this condition may have occurred before; however, I never noticed it before or after. There was so many fish I believe that you could stand on the bridge with a net and catch enough for a fish fry.

This bridge is the same one that I related to in perhaps in the very first paragraph. This bridge is located at the bottom of the hill on Bingham road, this route by using the bridge is the only passable way out Bingham road that is if you are located on the East side of the bridge. Well, I suppose a person could wade across the creek or perhaps jump across at a narrow spot in the creek when it is not flooded.

Sometimes it seems to me that I get to rambling on about things that are not so important, and I suppose to you they may not be either, but to me they are. It is weird how things keep popping into my mind. I sure am having fun with this. Whoops there it is again I got off track again I was talking about getting across the creek with out using the bridge. I would be wise to fore warn you that if you were to cross the creek by the means of wading you ought to take caution. Once you enter the muddy soil that is usually present on both sides of the creek it is infested with an abundance of little black blood suckers. These pesky little parasites really like to get attached to the tender skin between your toes; they really can get attached by somehow creating a hole in your skin where they can supply their body with life sustaining food. Oh, by the way, some of these critters take quite a pull to pry them loose and to a little person such as me it would hurt some when you pulled them loose. Are you surprised that I was able to recall some pain as a youngster?

While we are on the subject of the creek I want to share a time that my brother Bob and I had one summer day. It was a very pleasant day, nice enough to go play in and around the creek, I recall watching the older boys hunt for snapping turtles. Now if you're not familiar with these critters of the swamp, I can assure you they need to be respected. Let me explain, how that we, (I am now classifying myself as a *bonified* snapping turtle hunter), need to go over a couple of things that might be helpful in keeping yourself out of harm's way. Remember this was summer time; yup, no shoes, not a real good idea hunting snappers this way.

What we did was to go into the muck with our bare feet then we would trounce around in the mud until we located a turtle by stepping on it. Once we found one we would very carefully put our hands one on each side of his shell. Then all there is left to do is to lift him up out of the mud. At this point you have successfully bagged a trophy. I was just thinking, suppose a person was to put their hands in the wrong place. Ouch! One thing I should mention at this point, do not forget those little pesky blood suckers, by now there several on both feet. Now I have said all this, to get to the rest of the story, do you remember this whole thing was a set up to be able to let you hear what not to do with a snapping turtle? Here is what happened; I lifted the turtle up so that this proud and successful hunter could show off my special prize to my younger brother Bob. This really was not a real good thing to do because that snapper reached out and grabbed on to Bobs cheek! I don't think it broke the skin but you can be sure that Bob was really surprised and so was I.

There were a lot of things going on in our neighborhood. It may help to understand some of the things that went on could have been a little bit easier to understand, if we could grasp the whole makeup of the families that lived in our area. One thing to take into consideration is the decade that we are living in was during the years directly following the great depression. The people were very poor. Some of the folks were starting back to work as jobs were beginning to be more available. It is not so hard for a. person to understand that this was a very poor neighborhood.

Let us look at another factor that may help to see some of the predicament some of these folks have gotten them selves into. For instance, many of these families were large families, the Bigsby had nine living children, the Millers six, the Woolworths had…… I do not know how many, the LaValleys only had three kids. There were other families living in the area but not on Jameson Drive.

You know this seems to lead to a lot of possibilities of mischief going on, I just thought of something, suppose that an ice cream truck were to come along and it would be playing that come and get it music. This would be getting those that hear, thinking… my, it's hot; I sure would like some ice cream. Just think about that music, what a crowd of excited kids would be attracted by all of that inspiring noise. Well, you can forget all about that! First of all, they did not have ice cream venders that sold ice cream in this manner around this time, least wise not that I recall. However, there was something that we really got excited over. Can you grasp the over whelming joy we felt when Pa Jameson drove up in his old car, or perhaps it may have been a truck with a load of bakery goods! Just think of all the bake goods we could eat. Not only our family, but the whole neighborhood! I think it wise that I may need to share with you how it came about that our Grandpa happened on to this emasculate load of goodies. Well, it seems that Grandpa was raising a pig to butcher at a later date, and a local bakery would give to folks the items that they could no longer sale. Well, I am not sure how it came about but I will have to admit that some of the things were very delicious; especially to a hungry little boy. You could not eat everything especially the items that had mold on them but those that did not, yummy, yummy to the tummy. Exciting!

Chapter Two

This may be a new chapter but I will assure you, things they are related to are not really that boring. Now it is fairly obvious that the events that occur in this chapter are perhaps happening to a little older boy. Even the story about Bob and the turtle could have fit right into this chapter.

It is a little odd that most of the things I remember happened during the spring, summer or in the fall. This causes me to think that I may have some sort of mental deficiency .Why I am thinking that this could be is that I could not only recall the ***SUMMER TIME INCIDENT SYNDROME***. However, not being a doctor I am not really qualified to prescribe a pill to heal this disease that about one hundred per cent of us older folks have. Hey, I heard that snicker! Some of you younger people have the same problem, am I not rite?

There are some things that come to mind, such as the time our older brother Leon was sliding down the hill on Bingham road. This was without a doubt one of our favorite spots for sledding. Now, going back to Leon on his sled on the way down the hill with a full head of steam, I can just imagine the excitement racing through his body and perhaps, with his blood presser raised a tad, as he was approaching the bridge.

I feel as if there is a need to explain that when you are on ice it is rather hard to maneuver a sled as readily as you really need to. Well, with all the factors entered in, the hill, the ice, and the bridge and oh yes, let us not forget that the sled was a new one. (That may be why my sister Betty was so very upset when she found out the sled was completely demolished.) That's what happened alright, on the slide down, sure enough, Leon was unable to get clear of the bridge. I don't think that he sustained many injuries but that poor sled. It was a gonner. Actually, Betty was without a doubt more hurt than even the sled or anyone else.

No, here are a couple of more things that I would like to share with all of you. One is the time brother Harry ran around the house with no shoes on. Now I agree with all of you literary critics and there should not be any oos and ahs, however, that Harry done this at all wasn't unusual, he did it several days in a row. Now it seems that I neglected to tell you that what Harry was doing, that seemingly uneventful event, it did cause some issues. The area he ran around was most of the time covered with snow. Some days we would have as much as two feet or more of the white powder. It kind of puts a lid on the idea that this bunch was off their rocker a tad. Bare feet in snow! Well, Harry grew up to be one fearless football player when he reached high school, so I guess it did not hurt him a bit, to be crazy that is.

I just cannot understand how a person who grew up in Michigan cannot recall things that occurred in such violent weather. 0h, by the way, in later chapters as I have grown older, I am sure there will be more about the winter days. I almost forgot the latter part of the couple of items that I wanted to share what happened in my childhood days.

This particular story came about in April; it would be good to know that in April it is still pretty cold in the North. The story goes this way, my brother Milbert was going to set a tradition on his birthday; this was to go swimming on his birthday in the cold waters of the trussel. Now when Jim, I suppose that it is a good idea to explain that most people called Milbert, Jim, but I for one have always and always will, refer to him as Milbert. He set this goal; I am not convinced that when April came around on this particular year that there was a thin layer of ice on the waters of the trestle, so I am not sure that he went through with it. So if you want to you can finish the rest of the story.

Now that we have covered what my memory can produce about the winter times let us go back to some more summer time fun. But before we do there is something that just popped into my head. When there was plenty of snow on the ground, the hill on the west side of the bridge was a very nice slope to play on. We used just about anything that we could get our hands on to slide. An old car hood, a paste board box, a toboggan, maybe some skis. Oh, yes, I am not sure but somewhere in my recollection there was a sled mounted on some skis. I do recall though you had to be very careful not to come down the hill so fast that you're not able to stop before reaching the creek's edge, oh so very cold, if you happen to enter that icy water.

Chapter Three

Let us take a little closer look at this house that we so proudly called our home, I can see those big numbers that seemed so proudly to identify that tar paper shack. The number 2266 was the numbers that I recall so vividly.

Now tar paper shack may not be all that far out of an inadequate description of this mansion, it was covered with a heavy green tar paper or maybe it was roofing paper I am not sure. Whatever it was it covered in, the cracks that the boards left when the boards did not fit closely together allowed wind, snow, rain, mosquitoes, and perhaps many other things that we feel today to be very unpleasant to enter the house. If I have it right my memory only serves a limited picture, it seems as though there were two bed rooms, I do not recall a kitchen but there was a living room with a heater, which we did burn coal in during the winter. One thing that I recall that mentioning the stove brought to my attention is one day Milbert was heating up some coffee and he accidently spilled some hot coffee on himself and was burned very seriously. These are just some more things to bring out about the house to help you to see why, and understand why this house may have not been adequate enough for a family of this size. Of course it did not matter to the Bigsby bunch how we all got a good night's sleep, I don't believe there is any way to figure it out.

Just think I do not remember there being a chair, a couch, a table, a pot or pan, a dresser, or anything that would help aide in the setting up a house for housekeeping, that is with the exception of the two items that I had all ready mentioned one, the bed and the stove. Now I am not trying to say that there were none of these things in the house, I just don't recall them being there.

I am not sure if it would be possible for me to get across just what a great feeling that the tar paper was on a cold morning. Once the sun came up in the East, imagine even in Michigan the sun comes up in the East, I at many times would stand with my back to the tar paper wall in order to soak up some warmth. OH MY, did that ever feel good.

You know a house of this type often took a lot of abuse not only from the elements, but I will stress the fact that a lot of rug rats playing all sorts of rough house games can take a toll on any type of building. As time went on the ware and tare began to show up.

First, a small tear in the outside covering, tar paper, then another and another, well you get the picture. With this going on and no one doing any repairs, soon we have big problem. I may as well tell you about what took place pertaining to the house.

I never would have thought, even if I had been older and was able to understand what qualified for a suitable living quarters, or what was not. Now I have no evidence that what today, I suspect that someone may have leaked to the county, that the Bigsby house was not fit to raise children in. Now the house was condemned by the county and they gave Dad a certain amount of time to get it back in some sort of order. Now the amount of time is not something that I knew anything about but what I do know is this incident caused a lot of turmoil in our family.

First of all, I can remember we were practicing for our Christmas program at Bingham school when some county authorities came and got some of us and took us to a county facility. That's the way that I recall it, however it appears that they may have come to the house after school, anyway that is what may have happened it sure changed our life style. First of all Harry, myself, Bob, and Betty were sent to the county home to stay until the house was declared safe for occupancy. Duane who was not yet in school was allowed to go live with Aunt Mill and Uncle Evert. Uncle Evert was my mother's brother, he also was the son of Pa and Ma Jameson, of course my mother one of Pa's daughters.

Well let's go on with this fairly unpleasant tale.

Leon and Milbert were allowed to stay at home because they declared them old enough to maybe give some assistance in the repairs. Perhaps there is a question about what happened to Leroy? Well, it seems that I forgot to mention that Leroy had gone to live with Grandpa Jameson when he was just a baby. They say he was very sick so they thought that since there were so many children in the household already that he may have a much better chance of getting well.

    I will say one thing that really sticks out in my mind is the beds. Can you imagine enough beds for everyone? And it helps to know, in my whole life time up to this point. I have never had my own bed. It appears as though a person would be so ever grateful.

    However, if you only knew………..

This bed had bars that they raised up so that a small fellow such as I could not get out of. There was a slight feeling as though we were in jail. Now at this time I was probably about six years old. Can you grasp how that I felt? Not only me but the other three also? First of all we were away from the security of our freshly condemned home, being separated from our family, both those we left at home, plus the ones that came to the facility with us. We were scared; I think back and sort of cringe when I ponder on that very first night. I guess we sort of got used to being there because after that shocker, I can only recall one incident. That was when dad came to visit us on Christmas day. As plain as day, dad brought us a farm set it was an awesome present. I know this to be the first time that I can recall receiving a Christmas gift of this magnitude, however there may have been many before that I have forgotten about. Now that was not that important, because the next thing I recall is that we are back home again.

As I think about it there is a bunch that I don't remember. Like how long were we there, it must have been for at least six months. Now I find myself filling in the blanks instead of letting my readers do it. I can imagine that some of you folks can recall the facts better than I. If things happened the way that I have in my mind, they must have torn down the tar paper shack and replaced it with a basement house. Actually, I don't believe that they had finished it because I recall Uncle Everet for one, either got hurt or nearly died while he was doing something with a cement mixer. It seems as the mixer was operated, or maybe for a better word, powered by a gasoline washing machine engine. All of this is just secondary; the important thing is we are back and ready for some more summer time fun.

Chapter Four

Let us take a look at some of the things that us kids did for recreation. It did not take a lot of encouragement to get enough people together to form a decent game of **work up** going. (**Work up** is a game of softball where if you hit the ball and you are put out you go out to the outfield. You then have to make your way around to bat again.) The biggest problem that we had was if one of the neighbors who had a ball did not want to play, it may get to be a slight problem getting something to use for a ball. In other words, if you don't have a ball or the person who owns the ball gets mad, they can take it and go home!) I can recall the older boys would tightly wrap a rag and use it as a ball.

Another game that we really enjoyed playing was **Kick the can** this was perhaps a bit more hazardous than work up. It was probably more fun to play *kick the can* later in the evening because it was easier to sneak up and kick the can when it was a little darker. That way, the can tender (the guy that was it) may not see you in time and by the time he retrieves the can, everyone can escape to hide again.

There were other games that we played from time to time, I will name a few. In fact, most of the things that we were involved in are perhaps the same games as today's games. Of course your generation has some games today that in our day there were no monies to get equipment for. Allow me to list some that I can recall. To list a few such as, **dodge ball, kick ball, tug a war,** this was fun when you were to use the creek as the middle line, Oh yes! How about **King on the Rock,** this was quite the same as **King of the Hill.** Of course, the old classics such as **marbles, tag, hide go seek, Annie over, dodge ball, I draw a ring, and Red rover Red rover come over.** I have forgotten some but there surely was an abundance of things for us to do.

There were some things that I had not mentioned that was when we would sneak into Mr. Rairasons apple orchard and gather up drops. Drops are apples that fall off the tree; this is a process that nature has for thinning the apples when they are too many to grow properly. Now **apple wars,** as we sometime called them, were really not for the smaller kids because a person can get hurt when those apples hit you.

A chance to go to the movies was also great form of entertainment. I am going to tell you something that I am not very proud of. When I was a youngster I never thought a thing about what may have been transpiring. I knew that dad had frequently visited the local bar and I suppose that this was perhaps a normal thing.

Let me share with you what took place and to grasp the reasoning behind my thinking. This particular Saturday feature at the movie was a picture called **<u>Monsters of the swamp.</u>** I need to let you know how we felt and why that we felt as we did. More times than not when we got out of the movies it was getting dark; well, there was two ways to get back home after the picture show; one was to walk down Clio road to Bingham road then to the house. Now the distance may not be accurate but it seems to me to be close. I guess going this way was about two and one half miles. Now that is not all that bad. However, as you went down Clio road just outside of town there was a cemetery with very large oak tree overhanging the road. It was not many Saturdays before that the featured picture was about a black panther that was stalking a little boy and girl. This stuck to my mind very firmly. We were afraid that there was a Panther up in that tree! You are no doubt thinking what has this got to do with the way home? First let me share the other way home was to go down the railroad tracks, now this way was much shorter of the two. I would guess that this distance to be about one mile and a half. In order to reach home going down the tracks a person would have to pass over a trestle, and at night, this was a little scary for small kids. And that panther could be lying under waiting for us, so why worry? We were with dad so he would probably take care of us, right? Well, it seems as though dad enjoyed drinking so much, he would have us to walk home from time to time by ourselves.

This particular Saturday, all of us decided that we would not go to the movies but instead we would go to the dime store and spend our money on candy, then just hang around town until it was time for the movie to be over. It may have worked to, if our dad had not seen us from the bar stool. He was very upset, so then he gathered us up, and transported us to the house. I imagine that we were punished big time. .However I do not recall getting a whipping then or at anytime, I am sure that I got plenty of spankings, I just do not recall them. In the house, now that I can remember the bed for the very first time, this is where I was sent to for at least part of our punishment. I say this to say that five or six people lying on one bed was pretty crowded.

There is another incident, and there may be more that I feel that may be worth mentioning, as my mind may pick up on some thing that I wrote about or it could be one of those incidents that just pop up.

What I had in mind is something that took place at Mr.Raisons house. The Rairsons were very nice people. I can remember that they would invite us, and all of the neighborhood kids, over to take part in bible study. I don't recall them being too successful at it but at least they tried, this was a tuff group.

It was at the Rairsons that Mr. Rairson was doing some work around his cistern well and he was sharing some things about it and how it worked. Well, it did not take a whole lot to get this young boy overwhelmed. I was so interested in this source of water; it was not something that I had ever seen before. In fact, I cannot tell you where our water came from or even if we had any water. Well, back to the cistern.

I felt as though my little brother Duane needed to experience some of the same things and since I was now educated on these types of things, I was the one to show him. Well, I made another big booboo, when I lifted up the lid of that cistern and he peered into the well, he got too close to the edge and before we knew it, there he was laying face down in the water!

Now ole Ray knew that he had messed up. All I could was to holler and scream until the noise brought Mr. Rairson on the run. He took a hard rake and hooked it into either his belt or in his suspenders. He had no trouble getting Duane out of the well to safety. By the time that I quit making these stupid blunders and if I weren't to get smart enough, I am not sure there would be any of us left!

Come to think about this water thing, at our house I don't recall no electricity or plumbing. I know that the Millers down at the end of the road had electricity, running water, and an outside John. So, even though I don't remember, I would think that we did too.

When I mentioned the Millers something crossed my mind. Now the Millers are my mother's sister's boys, so this makes them first cousins. I am sure that being cousins did not make either party any better. All that I can tell is that there were just more kids to get into more trouble. By now we are probably around eight or nine years old. Bingham school is closed and now we attend Pine Run School, a much larger facility than Bingham school. Let me tell you the story that I was reminded of.

One afternoon some of us boys were playing around the railroad tracks; this is something that we did very often and we thought that it was great. When those big ole steam engines would come along; I can just feel the excitement that would possess our bodies and the thrill that we got when we would give them the high ball sign. Then when they got right beside us, they would turn loose a huge biller of steam and at the same time they would turn and blow that high pitch steam whistle. I can recall us kids would run for all that we were worth to get away from the steam, it was a thrill for us young ones, but I believe that it was great fun for those engineers too. Now it might be that some of you already know these old trains were fuelled with coal. Much of the cargo that they transported up and down the tracks with car loads and car loads of coal this was the main source most all means of the business world. It was not my intention to get off course with this short fact, since there is a lot of coal cars going up and down the tracks, there is also some spillage off the cars. Now this is free coal and we were to get as much as we could. It was understood that this was the thing to do... in fact it was a challenge to get as much as possible. This helped out a lot with the power bill during the winter months.

Now I was in the process of telling you about the time we were playing around the railroad tracks, there was a drain pipe under the tracks it was put there so that the water would not build up on the side of the tracks and perhaps build up so as to disrupt the train itself. Well anyway, when my cousin Don looked into the culvert he noticed a wild rabbit sitting in the pipe. This was all Dons idea! But the rest of us concluded that the plan was a good one. Here is what we did, Don went to the house and got his mothers new pillow case and left us other guys there to watch so that the rabbit did not run away. Something that I forgot to mention is that Don was also bringing with him Peter, now Peter was a large tame buck who had only three things on his mind, one is eating and I am sure to him this would take third place, number two and three would depend on rather this rabbit in the pipe was a another buck or if it were a doe. It is up to you to finish the rest of the story.

Now here is what took place. Don's brother and I were to hold the pillow case over the end of the pipe while Don released Peter into the pipe at the other end. Very little time lapsed from when Peter went into the pipe, the wild rabbit came flying out; well part of the plan worked but the part where the pillow case was to catch the wild rabbit didn't! The last time that we saw the wild rabbit, he was headed West with the peddle to the medal. When we examined the pillow case it had a hole in it about the size of that rabbit.

Perhaps these short incidents could have been placed in the areas with things that they could have readily linked up with. First of all in one of the stories, the one pertaining to my foot, remember mom carried me into the house? Now I am going to probably give you some information that I, for the likes of me, I do not understand. From this, no mater how much that I have tried, I can not remember a thing about mom until we moved to the farm in Oceana County. It seems that mom left dad and went to live with

Mr. LaValley. Well somewhere along the way, dad and mom got a divorce, and Ted and mom eventually got married. From this point I will refer to Mr. LaValley as Grand pa Ted.

Another thing that gets my attention, especially since Harry and I were talking about who it was that was responsible for a big fire down by the barn, I can remember this pretty well because with all this commotion it had all the neighborhood in an uproar. I can imagine that the folks knew that someone had caused the fire but they could not get anyone to own up to it.

Well, I will not keep you in suspense any longer; you see I have wondered what happened for quite a while. If the information is correct, Milbert was playing with matches down by the barn, and then with all the dry hay, **bingo** there she goes.

Then there was another time, which I for one did not think it to be all that spectacular, as the others made it out to be. (This story probably could have been entered into the paragraph that the games I told you about were in.) What caused this incident was dad must have gotten tired of all arguing and fighting between all of the guys and gals. So he went somewhere and purchased a pair of boxing gloves. Now the real reasoning behind this is that it may make it easier to control the problems that we were having with each other. Well this worked for some, but for Bob and Ray it turned out to be an ongoing catastrophe. Allow me to explain. Remember when two people get involved with personal differences, the rule was to put on the gloves and duke it out. Do you recall any one else putting on the gloves on other then Bob and Ray? Well I do not either, have you ever, or can you imagine, what it would be like if a person would throw a tom cat on top of another tom cat? Now this is what this boxing fiesta has turned out to be! The others would provoke the two of us into some sort of conflict; the result is here we go again. Now this has turned into a sporting event. Now Bob enjoyed it and so did the spectators but I assure you this is one fellow who did not! You see as I have already shared, with joy, that I was clumsy and slow. Now Bob on the other hand, was quick and fast, now you can finish the rest of the story…..

Now our time of living on Jameson Drive is about come to an end. There is one item that I think would be of interest to all of youins'. Since Bingham school has closed and we are assigned to go to Pine Run elementary, I am not really sure about this but it might have had something to do with the reason for the greatest failure in my life!

It happened like this, sitting in Mrs. Gilbreths third grade class room I noticed this very gorgeous blond girl whom I thought to be the Miss Universe of the twentieth century. Now I know that she had been there all the while, but I had never really noticed her. All of the sudden, I realized that this was the person that the Lord had planned for me to spend the rest of my life with. (Remember this is third grade!) When I finally mustard-up enough courage and wrote her a note and passed it to her, with the anticipation that I was fixing to hit a home run….. I mean a grand slam! Let me tell you what the profound note said, "I LOVE YOU, DO YOU LOVE ME?"

I can imagine that she may have felt as though Mr. America had just given her 20 dozen red roses…..and then you can figure out how I felt when she said NO. You know what **NO** means. This may have been the reason that I was so very shy, and also it was many years later before I could get enough courage to ask another girl to marry me. I will tell you all about it in the book entitled "Moms Garden".

Chapter Five

Well, the next thing that is happening is we are loaded in the back of a big truck. It was probably a one ton truck. On this trip, I do recall Milbert kept us occupied by leading us with the singing of songs like, **Zip a Dee Do Da, You are my Sunshine, 99 Bottles of Beer on the Wall,** and perhaps **She'lll be Coming Around the Mountain.** All of this singing helped in the passing of time. It was **very** cold so we bundled up with blankets and quilts or anything else that we could stay warm with. I am not sure at the time or how this arrangement came about, but we were heading for Oceana County. Now remember when I told you that the Pentwater River would again come in to play? Well, that is where we were heading. It was a long and tiring trip, but we finely arrived at Grandpa and Grandmas house that was setting right on the bank of the river. Now even though this house was not the greatest of houses, it was the place that they called home for so many years. I can imagine that I am now about ten years old. There is a lot of things to tell about, that were of interest that were connected to this house alone, one thing that really sticks out in my mind was that was a shallow water pump in the back yard. I think that they built a lean-to porch onto the house that extended over that same pump. The real reason I brought this up is to say, and those that remember will testify that this was so. The water was real cold that was pumped out of this pitcher pump. Very cold!! It was so good to drink from. The city boys were in the country now!

It was perhaps a touchy ordeal for us to get used to the change. We soon learned to make our way around and soon we were out there playing and rough housing as usual. The biggest difference here was that there was a lot more land, a lot of chores to do, and there was a lot less kids around to play with. There were only two houses where we came from and here there were about fifteen.

Grandpa Ted and my mother had gotten the use of a farm just down the road from Pa Jameson. I do recall the house was a two story building it was not in real good shape but a lot nicer than the basement house that we left in Clio. (It sure is great to be able to share the things I do recall, and think of those things a lot more readily.)

Let us take a look at who was now staying at what we will refer to as Grandpa Ted's house, now I have jumped way ahead of my self. It has just dawn on me that I had not started calling E.T., Grandpa Ted, until several years later. It has been brought to my attention that the eighty acres that Ted was farming was part of the land that PA had bought earlier.

I will not linger too long on this but as I recall there were Grandpa Teds three children Carl and Mary, and the third Norma, as I think back Norma was sent to Cold Water to a special facility to help cope with some issues that she had. Also arriving on the truck with Grandpa Ted were some of the Bigsby bunch Milbert, Bob, Betty, and myself. Now I assume that we had come to the farm perhaps in the early spring. The biggest clue to back up this assumption is that while we were getting settled we noticed that the **suckers** were running in the river. What we mean by the **suckers** running in the river is that the **suckers**, a medium sized fish around three to five pounds and as boney as all get out to deal with. Now I can just sense your mind working overtime thinking, if the fish are that boney what good are they? I will share this, once they are properly prepared, the small bones are edible. Also, they make a great fish patty.

As I was saying the suckers were running which means that they were coming upstream to spawn. I will share with you, but not only as a fact but as a warning, that this river is a trout stream and since it was a trout stream there was usually a game warden somewhere along the river. So a person needs to take precaution if you are going to fish the river as most of the river folks did.

Now fishing the river within the boundaries of the law was no problem; it was the method of fishing that caused some problems. Do you remember my cousin Don? Well, he is the one who introduced the method of using a spear as a fishing pole. What we did was climb out on an overhanging tree that had fallen down close to the water. Now there were always some of these trees for this was when the snow was to melt and the water in the river would over flow its normal path and come out of its banks, therefore causing the sandy soil to wash away from some of the bank exposing some of the roots, causing the tree to either topple in to the water or at least lean way over the water. Whoops! I got on a wild goose chase again.

I need to explain what happened to Harry. Well, it seems that Harry went to live with Grandpa and grand ma Bigsby, who only lived a few miles away. Duane was with Aunt Millie just across the way a couple of miles Leroy was still with PA and Leon must have stayed with dad. Oh well….my mind just follows whatever it thinks!! Can you keep up?

Let me go back and finish the story of illegal fishing. When you get out on the tree that is leaning over the water, the water is slowed down some. The tree blocking the flow of the water makes it clears so that a person can readily see the fish lying there just staying up with the current. This made the person doing the fishing, spear a fish successfully. Now I will say, this was a lot fun and this is something that I participated in several times while we were at the farm. It was fun until one day after I bagged a couple of fish, I noticed what I thought might be a game warden. I was not sure that he had seen me as I made my way up the bank of the river into the corn field as soon as I could. I discarded the spear in the corn field then I made my way to Pas house and threw the fish into the upstairs attic. I am not sure this maneuver was ever discovered but there is one thing for sure, I really was scared and more careful the next time that I went fishing. Cousin Don was always telling about the time when the big trout would come up the river to spawn, how it was a great thrill to spear one of them. Now this was in the forties. Later they planted Coho salmon in to Lake Michigan and now they come up the river to spawn as well.

Chapter Six

Well that first summer on the farm was a great time for us to have a fun time and for us to learn a little responsibility and respect; not only for the adults but for each other also. That first summer was a mixture of work and play. Actually, we were required to get our chores done before we could have playtime.

Out behind the house was a barn, much larger than the lean-to shack that we had on Jameson Drive, in fact this one had a large hay loft where the hay to feed the animals was stored. It seems that Ted would go to someone else's farm and cut their hay on halves. Then bring the hay to the barn and then store it in the loft. Now there were a lot of uncertainties of who owned the team of horses that we were using to cut, haul, and pull the hay up into the barn. I wonder if it might be of interest to you folks to understand a little bit about this procedure.

Well after the hay is cut, we used a horse drawn sickle mower to cut the hay, and then you let it lie on the ground until it dries, probably about three days providing that it doesn't rain and the temperature is a determining factor also. I can recall watching them hitch the horses to the dump rake, going along the freshly cut and dried hay with the horse drawn dump rake and then when they felt there was enough hay in the rake, they would dump it in a pile, and then lower the rake again until the whole field was raked in piles. Now it is time to load the hay onto the wagon, and this hay had to be loaded on the wagon by hand. There were three tined pitch forks used for this purpose. The only step left is to get the hay up into the loft of the barn. To do this brings on the horses again, what you need now along with the horses is a long strong rope and three blocks. Some folks refer to these as block and tackle. Now you place one block at floor level, one block high near the top of a gin pool and at the end of the swing pole. Then they would string the rope through the blocks then attach a hay fork, especially made for this purposes. Now you are ready to hook the horses to the rope, jam the special fork into the wagon load of hay and say, **"Getty up"** to the horses. Now with very little effort the horses pull a lot of the hay up into the loft. Now you swing the pole to where you want to dump the hay, pull the dump rope then repeat the process. There is one thing I forgot to mention <u>the dump</u> rope is a small rope hooked to the fork and when you pull it, it releases the hay.

There are a lot of things that took place during those couple of years that we spent with mom and Ted. We had a great time playing around the barn and rolling tires was perhaps the most fun .Oh don't get me wrong it was also a lot of fun when we would go to the swimming hole, located down river from Pa Jameson's house This was a great spot a high sand bank that over looked the river that is making a quick turn causing a little deeper hole than in the rest of the river. It sure was fun playing **king on the hill** at the ole swimming hole. This water was really cold as some of you know a spring fed river always is, sort of like a quick freeze. It makes your feet hurt- you dive in it. Get wet in a hurry. When you are wrestling and playing hard and getting hot then someone sends you into the water this is a real shocker.

The first summer was great; there were not a lot of things going on until around September, the farm is set for the winter. The first school season was fixing to start. I must have had another failure of the brain because only one thing do I recall about Saint Mary's school and that is the little pot bellied stove that sure felt good to stand around when it was cold. Saint Mary's school was about one and one half miles from the farm. I am sure that in winter we had to contend with a lot of snow. Remember they did not use busses for country schools at this time. I suspect that is why Mason County placed schools at regular intervals, I guess to cut down on children walking to school more than a couple of miles. So when your parents talk about walking to school in the snow…..remember how you thought they were making it up? I didn't. Sure wish that school that was close was still standing, but it was long gone! So walk we did.

It may have been this fall or it may have been the next summer that we got an opportunity to pick up potatoes for a local farmer, and get paid for it too. I have no idea how much that we got paid for picking up the potatoes, but I guess that it was 3 to 5 cents a bushel. This does not appear to be very much; however it was probably the going rate. I would like to share this fact, this was the first time that I can recall having money of my own, not counting the dime dad use to give us to go to the movies.

With this money we made working for Mr. Monton become a life changing experience. How times have changed, I am now about ten years old; it has dawned on me, how come as most of you know that I have a great fondness for probably my greatest vice. If I were to ask you what you think this vice was. Some would reply diet coke. Well, this is wrong. On this particular day someone, probably Ted, carried us to the store. We had money, so I introduced my self to an ice cold RC cola! My, what a mistake that was, if I had all the dollars that I spent on RC I may not of had to pick up that last bushel of potatoes. Just imagine the very first store bought cold drink you have ever had! I guess that may have started a revelation in me, for when we would pass Bucks Corner it was again time for another RC.

      As I ponder on the idea of making our own money the more I determined that this was a great idea. There were several things that we did especially in the harvesting of money crops. In the next three or four years we will have involved ourselves in farm related labor jobs. By the way if a person is in school they were excused from school to work.

Now I pause long enough to let you know that this type of work was at times not so pleasant. I am referring to the time while we were picking up potatoes. I am not sure that you are familiar with how the routine was when you process the harvesting of the potatoes. After the farmer takes a one or two roe digger; he digs as many potatoes as he figures that his **picker uppers** can pick up the next day. Well this particular night, it came about a 3inch snow, now this was cold on the hands. This was the last crop to be picked before winter.

There were three or four crops we could make money at and I guess that it is time to get back to the list. Now this list may not be in the order in which they occurred, but this is to show you what we did to earn a little cash. Now in the spring, there was strawberry picking, sweet cherries, sour cherries, pickles; many times we would pick pickles on half's. When you do this you have to have means to haul the pickles to the market, now there were peaches, apples, currents, blue berries, and prunes. Most of these are things that I myself involved in doing, I am not sure that all the family was involved. Also some of these took place sometime up until, and including, my first year of high school.

Now I would like to share a few things that still linger on my mind, one is, I still have that mental lapse when it comes to things that took placed in the winter time. Not a lot happened during the winter that I can recall with the exception of a couple of things. Now this was the first year and the last one that we spent with mom on the farm. The things that I was thinking about, is this. It would be good to know that the farm was located about half way up the Lower Peninsula and about five miles from the Lake Michigan lakeshore. Now if you know much about the great lakes you may realize that is potential for a lot of lake induced snow storms. Now suppose that the main or only source of fuel for both cooking and heat is wood. Now in this area there is woods everywhere, that is in the early forties. A smart squirrel will store up acorns and anything else that might be able to be used for food to be able to survive the cold winter. Now I am thinking about the storing up of wood for the winter. Anyhow there were a lot of woods available, it seems Pa Jameson had purchased 160 acres originally, and then I am thinking maybe another 80 acres, which is the farm that we were living on at this time.

Now let us go back to the gathering of the wood for the winter. I do not recall how they got the wood to the house but it seems that we used the same buzz saw to cut it and that I have that same saw in my barn now, but I don't use it. I do recall that they would take the wheel off the old model A truck then put on one that had no tire on it. Then to motivate the saw to turn they would put a belt between the tireless wheel and a drive pulley that was attached to the same shaft that the big round saw was on. Now this pulley was about 6 inches wide they would take a flat belt put it on the wheel, give it a half twist then put it on the drive pulley. Now all there is to do is to crank up the old truck, then by using a hand throttle, pull out the throttle to the desired speed, now you are ready to cut the fire wood into the proper length. I am assuming that the men folks and the older boys were in charge of the sawing then it was up to us younger folks to stack the wood into stacks. I am sure the way we were to stack the wood was called cording. By putting the wood stack 4 feet high and a few feet long provided a good way to locate the wood when the big snows came later.

Now that the wood is cut and piled there is very little work to be done the rest of the winter. Well we still have our daily chores to do. Things such as feeding, and watering the animals, cleaning the stalls, gathering the eggs, get wood in and maybe split some for the cook stove, that's about all there was to do. Of course we still have to go to school. I do not remember us kids being involved in school just the warmth of the stove. Ted and…….. Oh, Carl, he would cut popular trees into about six foot lengths all for the paper mill, this ways to make a little extra cash.

One more thing that I would like to mention is that we had a couple of cows and they had to be milked, this was done by Carl. Come to think about it, I don't recall Carl going to school at all this winter. He may have gotten old enough to quit school. I do recall that we had all the milk that we wanted. I can remember that there was a cream separator and once the cream was separated from the milk, the milk left over after feeding the calf's it was free game.

Something I said may be still lingering on in your mind, separator, what is that? All that I can tell you that it is a machine that has a lot of parts: one big bowl, two spouts, and a handle. Now all you do is pour the milk into the bowl, then turn the handle and as you turn it, milk will come out one spout and the cream out the other. We know what happened to the milk but what about the cream? Well, it seems as though Ted had conspired with a creamery in Scottville to buy the cream. This is what many of the farmers did for some cash money. Well, you need to know that mom saved out enough cream to make butter with. Now I seem to remember that

Grandma Jameson had a butter churn to make butter with. However, my mom used a two quart jar to make it in. I will never forget shaking and shaking and shaking then bumping and shaking it some more until the butter starts to gather, then finally, you have unsalted butter. After mom gets through with it you have a very good spread.

Now it is time to get back to the story. Our second summer on the farm was a real trip, as you will find out. I can recall, after the ground was ready to plant, that means the soil is turned over or shall we call it plowed under, either way you still have to disc or drag it with a harrow until it is rather level. Then there was the next step; we had to mark the rows. By now you are thinking we must be preparing to plant some sort of a row crop, you are so right. The name of the crop is field corn. Now field corn is usually grown for the purpose to use for feeding the animals. However, when it is tender it makes a very palatable .Even when the corn is very young we would go a corn stalk, pull off an ear and eat it cob and all!

Now back to the planting of the corn. To give you some perspective of what sort of job that was looking us in the face, this is a pretty good size patch of corn. Anyway let us take a look at what the procedure was to mark off the field before the planting starts. It takes two people, a long pole about ten foot long, and five three foot lengths of chain and finally, five pieces of rope that you can hook the chain to the pole. Now the first rope will be tied to the pole at the two foot mark then the second rope at the four foot mark and so on until all the ropes are attached, Now what's left is the two people position themselves, one on one end of the pole and one the other end. The one on the right is the one that the responsibility of keeping the rows straight. We will call this person the **A** man and the other the **B** man. The **A** man sites a spot on the far side of the field and the purpose is to keep his eyes focused on that spot and walk straight towards it. Now the **B** man has to keep up with the **A** man and as they walk across the field they will have left behind them five easy to see fairly straight marks in the soil. Now the next step is to swap the pole around so the **A** man is next to the last mark on the field, now he can use the mark as a guide line. They keep repeating this process until the field is finished and is done going one way then set up the sane and go across the field the other way. When you have finished you will have a field marked off in a square pattern. Once marking is done, then you get planters, and one at a time you take a row and plant the seed into the ground, you try to plant the seed right on the mark. Just in case you are not familiar with the by hand planters, which were better then the old method of digging a hole with a hoe ,placing the product into the hole, then covering it up with the loose dirt to complete the process. The planters that we used had two handles, a hand grip on each handle, and a type of metal container to hold the seed in. All there was to do is place the point of the planter into the mark that were made earlier, then with a motion to the left with the handles to allow the corn, just enough for one hill, then move the handles to the right so as to deposited the corn into the ground Now there is nothing to do, except do this same thing over and over until the field has been planted.

Now after this boring process that we just went over I believe we need to go on, even though this may have been interesting to some of you it may not have to others. Now this was a hot job and water was the only thing to drink. It meant we either had to go to the river or to Pa's house to get a drink. Either place the water was real cold.

Now I don't know for sure just who did it ………but the day was long and we were very tired, anyway when we ran out of seed, we were so very glad it was time to go to the house for supper. Now I told you this, you can once again fill in the blanks. When the corn came up there was a bunch of corn come up in a big pile I wonder what might have happened; now it is your turn again fill in the blanks.

There were some things we did rather than work all the time. I remember that we would go down the dirt road to where it ended in a two track road like a trail where people would dump their trash. We would entertain ourselves plundering through the stuff hoping to find something interesting to play with or find something useful. Now for some reason I enjoyed finding those *Zink jar lids* and breaking the glass out of them. As a kid it did not really matter a bit, they were thrown away so that's good enough to classify them as trash. Now to give you an idea where I am going, a couple of summers ago I paid 25 cents apiece for several of these lids and was glad to get them.

Chapter Seven

I was very mixed up for a while. But that isn't unusual is it? Now on to the next story.

I could not figure out just how my brother Leroy had a car and for the likes of me I was getting more confused. I was thinking that if you had to be 16 in order to get a drivers license. Aunt Pearl and I were talking about this and she shared with me that since he was the only one living with Pa and Grandma Jameson they got him a liscens at the age of fourteen. Now I feel better about telling this story, I recall going with Leroy and his driving several of us kids around we would jump on or in his **Model A Ford** convertible with a rumble seat and headed towards Pentwater. Our intent was to go to the movies. Now this was at a time that there were no jobs, for there was no extra money to go to the movies with. As we travel towards Pentwater we watch the side of the road for pop bottles. From the time that we had left the house with those bottles that we gathered at the house and the bottles that we found along the road we would most of the time have enough to get into the movies. I also remember stopping at a little gas station to get gas. What stuck out in my mind was the method of pumping the gas; they had a *hand operated pump.* It had a five gallon glass container at the top. The glass container had markings on it to indicate how much gas that you needed to purchase. If you wanted two, three, or as much as five gallons, you take the pump handle, pull it back, and then push it forward until the gas reaches the line that indicates the desired amount. All there is to do is put the nozzle into the tank, squeeze the handle, then the gas, and by the use of gravity allows the gas to pour into your tank. I sure wish I had one of these pumps today.

I would like to sort of sum up the two summers that we spent at the farm. There is, I imagine, that I perhaps, even though I believe at this time am eleven years old, I learned some very important work ethics. I learned that it was good to have a partner, rather it was work or crime, it was better to work together to have a better chance of success. Now I can tell you are thinking crime….. What is that all about? Now before I go any farther, I would like to disclose to everybody whom I'd like to partner with. Now I chose Mary because I felt that she would do her share of the work, also when we were doing piece work she had very similar work ethics and was probably at least as fast as, or maybe faster than I was.

Now some of you probably know that I may not be all that fast but I gave it my best effort, also, I would rather work by myself when it comes to piece work. But when you have someone like Marry to work it turns out very well. (It takes two to harvest potatoes because the rows are too wide, and two for fishin' one to watch for the game warden!)

I also would like to pay some special thanks to my mom, I never really gotten to know my mom until this stay on the farm. She was a very caring lady and she could cook too. Being a farmer's wife with several working kids there was a lot of cooking going on. There is something that all of you may not know. One day while she was washing clothes in that old gasoline washing machine, mom must have caught her arm in the ringer. Now for those that don't know, the ringer was an apparatus at the top of the washing machine, designed to squeeze out the excess water out of the clothes once they were washed. The result of catching her arm in the ringer was a broken arm.

Another flash that may be interesting to some is that sometimes we went without shoes at the farm there were a lot of sandspurs, so even though our feet were tough, it was kind of wise to wear shoes. Sand spurs, sand vetch, and milk weed weeds were some of the things that readily grew well on the soil at the farm. Oh, do you remember the plant we called belly buttons? Most certain this is not their real name, we did eat them however. (Yuck, by Lou Ann) Also, it was kind of interesting how good and sweet that the sand vetch blossoms were, not only them but also the clover.

Another thing that has slipped my mind is something that we really enjoyed doing and that is going frog hunting. We have caught a lot of frogs in our days at the farm. There were two means we might have used besides catching them with our bare hands. Using your bare hands allowed too many of them to get away. Using a spear was another way but I always used a club to get their attention. Actually, this most of the time knocked the attention out of the frog .We hunted frogs also when we lived on Jameson Drive, but there it was hard to get someone to cook them. However, at the farm there were more people that would cook them for us. Boy, they were sure delicious fried in butter. It seemed that there was never enough to allow everyone to get their fill but everyone got some.

There were a couple of more things that were a first time things in my life that I can remember. One thing is the first time I had gotten on a ***cleetrack*** tractor. This was the tractor used in the woods when Ted was working with the pulp wood. The other thing occurred later so I will have to tell you about it in the book Mom's Garden. You will hear more about frogs in Mom's Garden too.

Chapter Eight

Well, we left the farm in the late summer when I was still eleven. I think that our Dad had sent the money for bus fare. My guess is that dad moved and sent for us, it seems that he left Jameson drive and had moved to a house just off Corona Road. Some that came along on this trip were Milbert, Harry, Bob, Betty, and myself. Now this must have been some sight, five children, one 16 year old and the rest under the age of 12. The instructions were to go to Flint and get off at the main bus terminal down town. Then catch the Corona Road city bus and take the bus to the end of the line. Then it was not very far to the street that we were now going to be living on. There was no one there to meet us so we had to make out the best that we could. Milbert had the address written down. I am not sure whether it was a policeman or if it were someone who just wanted to help, but anyway this person helped us to find the house.

There are a few things that I recall happening during the stay at this nice house; well it was nicer than most places that we were used to living in. I really did not like living there because we have always lived where there was plenty of room to roam. We did not know it at the time, but we only stayed at this house in the city until spring. I got sort excited on our stay here, we had the opportunity to go trick or treating for the very first time, now this was a treat. I have never had so much candy of my own. What was so neat about that is that everyone else had a lot too. This meant we didn't have to share. But what was really good is we had fun just trading the kind of candy that we don't like for the kind that we do like. What an experience!

Leon had always stayed with dad and was still with dad when we came to live here. I can remember while we were here he started going to go to Utley High school, I am not sure but the name of the school that we went to was probably Utley grade school. It was probably about a mile walk to school. Dad must have been doing rather well at this time because I can think back to some times that he would give us a nickel and tell us to go by the store and buy us a fruit of our choice for school. Somehow or somewhere I had tasted an orange before and it must have been good to me, because every time I had the chance my nickel went toward an orange. Now I suppose that as it is today, the oranges were all wrinkled up then, that's the way they are today in the stores. They sure tasted good swiveled up or not.

I also recall going to church, that is if my memory serves me right. Milbert started going to this small church and this one time, they gave the person that brought the most people for the first time, a prize. Milbert got some of us kids to go with him. I am not for sure but I think that he got a picture prize. That was another first; however I did go back a couple of times more.

Another thing that I remember is that dad had a side job. What he was doing was unloading coal out of the railroad coal cars. I understand that they were to get paid by the car load, they unloaded. At times dad would unload a car by himself then at times Leon would help. My, was that ever a dirty job.

Now I have only one more thing to report on during this brief stay here in the city, actually it was in the outskirts of the city that this incident took place sometime during the winter. Now this is something I definitely would not encourage anyone to try. I hitched a ride on the bumper of a car. I will say this driver had no idea that I was there. The sled on which I was riding was doing great until the car turns onto Corona Road. Now if I had known what was to take place I would have let go of the bumper. An icy road was a smooth ride and I thought I'd have more fun if I stayed on. What created my greatest concern was when the runners on the sled met the part of the pavement that was not covered with ice. They had salted the road and the ice was gone! The sparks were just a flying. Here I am scared to let go and scared to hang on. After a little ways we hit some more ice and I let go. After getting to safety, I decided that trick was stupid and I decided never again would I try that stunt. Now that I am 75 years of age I so far have kept that promise.

Chapter Nine

Well, school is out and we leave to go back up north. Now I don't know if this was a planned out move or if it were something like…. let us go and see what happens? There was a period of time that what happened is a little fuzzy and I just do not know how to fit it together. I do recall that one thing or a part of what took place. For one, I went with Harry when he went back to Grandma and Grandpa Bigsby. It was here that I learned a lot of values. Now lets take a little closer look at two people who have many different ways living in the same house .Grandpa Bigsby was a person who had a way about himself that others who did not know him may think that he was obnoxious.

Now before I go any farther, I want to tell you a little bit about Grandma Bigsby. Grandma was very religious and sort of old fashioned. Never had I seen her, that she ever wore anything but a long, grandma dress, she wore no make up, and she did not need it. Grandma was a very good cook and she was pleased when you were to compliment her on the preparation of and the awesome taste of her great food. Grandma went out of her way to please her husband. I think it was mainly because she loved the Lord so very much. She was a regular attendee of a local Presbyterian church. Since there were times that grandpa would not carry her, which was not very often. There were times that Harry and I would go to church with her, but I don't recall a time that grandpa went with us. Now I cannot judge if a person is a Christian or not, but his actions while I knew him did not display what a Christian should be like. Of course I was not a Christian either but I could see when someone was possessed with a mischievous nature.

There were a couple of things that took place that I would like to mention before they slip my mind. One of the things was it always seemed so good when Grandpa Bigsby would suggest that we make some ice cream. This is again the first time that I can recall making ice cream. Also, it might have been the first time to eat ginger snaps, which Grandma Bigsby seem to have when we had ice cream. At first they tasted strong but after awhile they had a taste that sort of grew on you.

Some of the things that my Grandpa Bigsby did that he really liked to do was for one, he would put out his hand, his fingers cuffed and say, "here", as if he were handing you a fist full of money, then when you responded by holding out your hand he would drop in to your hand a chewed up wad of tobacco. (Gross) I will never forget he always chewed **Peerless** or **Redman** brand tobacco. Another thing that I recall Grand Pa Bigsby doing, is singing this song, "In the sweet bye and bye give me some pie, I will meet you on that shore, give me some more." Now, I really think that he only sang the song this way when Grandma could hear it. He really enjoyed trying to agitate her. Another thing of interest is Grandpa had some pretty neat toys. Those of you that are my age probably will recall the old cars and trucks that were made out of cast iron. These cast iron toys were a far cry from the wooden blocks that we had available to play with. There were also some cards that we would play with; that up until that time, I had not seen nor have I seen since. I don't recall the name of the game nor do I know how that we played the game. One other thing that really gave Grandpa Bigsby a kick start, was to get the kids together then take a hand full of pennies, toss them out and watch the kids scramble after the coins.

Never have I been in a two story barn, this was pretty neat to an eleven year old boy who had but only two summers of farm experience. The top story not only would store the hay but there is adequate space where equipment could be stored. Tools and personal items is what Grandpa Bigsby kept there. To me this was a big barn! Now I will admit that I have seen big barns but was never in one. Below the top story of my Grandpa Bigsby's barn he had his hand tools and several mechanic parts he had put in there for safe keeping. Oh yes, the story goes that he also had a bottle of whiskey hid in that room somewhere that he liked to frequent, fairly often. Now he was not so fond of the room, other than for the booze being in there. Like I said, he went to the room when he felt that he needed or maybe he just wanted a snort. Now he would just not go back to the house, he would just hang around the barn or go to the garden, or perhaps wander down toward the springs.

Speaking of the springs, it reminded me of the time that grandma sent me to get a couple of kettles of drinking water which she used for cooking too. Now I am not sure that all of you know this but there was no running water at Grandpa Bigsby's house at this time, so we got the drinking water from the springs down by the creek in the pasture. Now there were two rail gates that I had to climb through to get to the springs, on the way back with the water, not being real careful because I really was not overjoyed about this chore, I accidently bumped the rail and put a ding in the aluminum pot. Now this may not seem all that serious but Grandma had just bought these pots and in my mind I sure thought that maybe I should prepare for a lashing but thankfully not much was said.

Do you ever watch the early American movies? Remember how that they would put a wooden barrel under the eves of the house in order to catch water in to have water for washing and bathing or anything that may come up that you might need water for. We did that too.

You know we mentioned a little while ago how good a cook that Grandma Bigsby was? Well, I guess that I ought to tell you how that Grandma done a lot of baking. This included baking her own bread, pies, cakes, or whatever else that was needed to satisfy the wants and needs of her family.

Oh my, I almost forgot to mention whenever Grandma baked bread she would also bake the most delicious yeast rolls that have ever entered this eleven year old boy's mouth! It makes you want to slap your Grandma with a great big kiss! Now to make it even better, throw on the roll a heaping helping of her home churned butter, Oh, I am sure glad they had not thought of dieting at that time.

Another thing maybe I ought to mention is that there was always a very large garden and out of this garden came enough vegetables to eat fresh while they were in season; and there was plenty for canning in preparation for the winter months. They also raised plenty of sun flowers so as to allow the birds to have something to eat.

I recall one summer they raised one hundred white longhorn chickens to eat and to can for later. Now I'm not sure when I went back to dads……. but guess its time, for me to move on. However it was not very far to the farm that I moved on to, I guess about two and a half miles from Grandpa Bigsby's.

Chapter Ten

I will admit that I was sort of glad to be back at home with the family, not that Grandpa Bigsby was not family but there was more kids at dads and all my life I had always been around lots of children. Well, let us take a look at this so called 20acre farm.

At first it was great; there were five or six acres of fruit trees. There were sweet cherries, sour cherries, and prunes. Now I am not real sure, but there may have been another kind of fruit besides the ones affore mentioned. No matter, when you grow this many types of fruit, you can't call it a money making venture. The entire orchard was in one corner of the property and in the opposite corner was about three acres of a fruit called currents. I can remember help picking them; however, I am not sure what they did with them whether they took them to the market, or just what they did do with the currents. I do know that they are very sour and most people made jelly with them.

Now let us go on with the lay out of the farm. There was a fairly large two story house. A large barn and a chicken coop located to the rear but sort of centered between the house and the barn. If you can imagine this, there were a few apple trees around the chicken coop and toward the back of the house. Now the apple trees, even though there were just a few, will turn out to be very important.

First of all there was a very large black walnut tree in the front yard. No running water in this house either, but there was a pump outside towards the barn. This pump kind of reminded me of the type of pump that they used with a wind mill. With no running water in the house it is obvious that the bathroom facilities are on the outside of the house. The location of the **two holer** was just to the edge of the lean-to that was attached to the side of the barn.

Now let us take a closer look at this two story farm house. Downstairs there were four rooms, two bedrooms, a living and dining room combined, and a kitchen. On the back there was a small room that today we would probably call a washroom, however we just piled junk in it. Now up stairs there was, I think, three more bedrooms, two of which were small and one was pretty large. There was a closet the full length of the house. This was a good set up with everyone having a bed to ourselves; keep this thought for just a little while.

Down below the current patch, I call it a patch for the lack of knowledge of what they referred a current patch, or whatever, it is called, there is a fairly large gulley, I will return to the gulley at a later time.

Not knowing for sure and since the family had already been living at the farm I would assume that dad got the farm already furnished with the necessities to start farming. This must have not only been the house furnishings, but also a team of horses, a cow and some equipment to do the farming with. I am not saying this to belittle my father, but in my mind, which is and was not really up to par, cannot imagine him trying the profession of farming. However, he did and we're glad that perhaps we have finally settled down in one place for awhile.

I do not recall putting up any hay for the animals for the winter, there was already some in the barn when I got there so I guess that had been seen about. There was around five acres of corn planted and it was growing pretty well.

Now not being all that experienced in driving a team of horses it was left up to Bob and I and Milbert to get the farming done. Now Bob and I could do a lot. Milbert was more of an inside person. Getting him to do outside work really took some doing. I suppose you are wondering where Leon is at? Well, I am not for sure but he must be about eighteen years old and I know that he enlisted into the Navy at a young age. I believe his enlistment was for six years. However, if I am wrong, I will stand corrected.

Now the summer was passing by rather quickly, most of the farming as far as preparation for a crop was done, if it were to get done, because the planting had to be done in the spring time. Now the cherries should have been already picked. I guess what was not eaten by the kids was gotten by the Robins. In case you did not know it, the beloved state of Michigan selected for its state bird the Robin. I Believe the Robins favorite food is cherries. Well, this may not really be a fact, but they do eat a lot of cherries.

Later in the summer it is time to pick currents, however I am not sure what they did with the currents, the prunes were pretty scattered but they were the next fruit that was ready. We did not even pick them except to eat. Now I will say this, those prunes were very good especially after the fall came and it got cooler and the prunes got riper. You cannot imagine how sweet that they were.

Do you remember that I had said something about the apple trees that were out around the chicken coop? Let me tell you how they had a part in our farming enterprise. For one thing, in order to grow apples without the meat enclosed was to spray them in order to keep the worms from getting into the apples. Well I am not sure, but I have a sneaky suspicion that these apples had not been sprayed in awhile. This means that these apples were not any good for the fresh fruit market. But, do not fret, all is not lost, there is still the cider mill. I do not to this day know where the truck came from but we gathered up all the apples that we could muster. Now it mattered not if they came off the tree or off the ground. Yep, you guessed it, no matter if they had worms or if they were not yet ripe, it did not make a difference if the apples were rotten. They were taken to the cider mill and dumped in with other green, wormy, and rotten apples. Then put through a squeezing to extract the juice out of the apples to make cider or whatever else they did. The money that we took in was not a lot, perhaps maybe ten cents a bushel. Not too bad considering that gas was probably around fifteen cents a gallon. Not so very bad considering that the prunes brought in nothing at all.

It is now approaching time to go to school once again. Most times starting a new school can at least, if the person is shy can usually cause some anxiety to the new student, because that person does not know the other people. Well this usually is the case; however we knew someone who was going to Butler school. This school was actually known as West Riverton public school. Now the person that we knew was our brother Harry, who has been, and still is staying with Grandpa Bigsby; their house located about a mile to the north. Now I had gotten acquainted with a cousin named Gene Golf. Now if you stop reading this so called book you will fail to find out what happened when we really got acquainted and I mean really got together. So do not give up and learn about something I never, ever did again!

School at Butler was a real trip. For those that are not familiar with the country schools that were available in the thirties and forties, you never knew that they were probably two room school houses. Of course at time, there were not enough students or maybe perhaps not enough teachers or even it could be that the poor maintenance failed to keep one of the rooms open. It so happens, that Butler school had two rooms with one teacher. Mr.

Farrell was our only teacher so we did not use the extra room; one room, one teacher.

Now I had mentioned that going to school at Butler was a trip, do you remember that? For one thing Mr. Farrell ……. Oh, I just thought of something I had heard a couple of others in their conversation to each other say…… old man Farrell. So with my country boy ignorance thought that it must be o.k. to call him **old man Farrell**. Well, one day at recess, I, unassuming that I was about to make a great mistake, replied to his jest of acknowledgement, that I was a new student and he wanted to be my friend. Well, I also wanted to be his friend, so I thanked him and simply replied, "thank you old man Farrell." Mr. Farrell walked in to the school house and I went back to playing ball with the rest of the kids. Well, in a very few moments, Mr. Farrell came back out of the schoolhouse and called out my name. And, with a stern voice demanded that I should come to where he was at. Perhaps I should have known, by the sound of his voice that this may have been something rather than a kiss on the cheek. It was a smack on the cheek all right, however the smack was with his open hand that sent this unsuspecting seventh grader sprawling on the ground for everyone to see. Now I did get over this **best school experience** that I could ever have. Maybe the experience was not all that great but the lesson that he taught me was great. I apologized to Mr. Farrell and we got along very well after that. Now this very important lesson has remained a vital impression on my life all 79 years of it.

Mr. Farrell was a great teacher, he always had my attention, I wonder why, and we learned a lot from him, can you, in your mind imagine how it would be to teach a class with two eight graders, now add three in the seventh grade, how about one in the sixth, four in the fourth, two in the second grade and after all this, put four first graders in the room all together? It takes a special teacher to baby sit such a wide range of youngsters with such a wide range of learning skills. To be able to control a group of children of this size must have been a real job, not alone to teach them some book learning. Now I will admit, that most of the things that I retained was the math and I particularly liked the addition. I don't really remember but he probably put the younger students working on their lessons, then he would spend a lot of the time with the older classes doing math. Mr. Farrell would first start out with a single line of digits, as he put them on the board he expected you to know the answer. Then he would put up a row of two digit numbers, then three, then four. Now once that a person does this enough it should help them to not depend on a cash register to count the money for them. Not like today, anyway.

I would like to let you in on a piece of information that some of you do not already know. Mr. Farrell was a farmer in the summer and a teacher the rest of the time. With this in mind, it will help you college trained teachers, to perhaps understand what it took to get teachers during the war time years. Now I am not saying that today's college trained teacher is not great, what I am saying however is that these teachers that were pressed into the teaching profession were a whole different breed.

Now that we are on the school bit we might as well finish with the items pertaining to the incidents that happened in and around the school. One thing that I recall is that anyone old enough, providing they had a job with permission, would be excused from school to help the farmers with their crops. It is not too hard to understand why most of the older boy and girls missed some time when there were crops to be harvested. What I want to

81

say here is, and I will tie it in with school, that we lived about four miles from Lake Michigan. With this in mind when you live this close to the lake during the winter you are most of the time are going to get a lot of lake snow. Now here is why I brought this up, go back to when I said that Mr. Farrell was a farmer. Now if you are a farmer and a school teacher and you have to be in the school so many days during the school year then it is very important that you do not miss any days, The reason that I say this is because, if you miss days then you have to stay longer in the spring therefore cutting into some very vital farming time. So to eliminate that possibility, Mr. Farrell would put on his snow shoes and walk, as he did the whole school year, he had the distance of two and a half miles from his house to the school. Now I want you to think a moment about this, if there is that much snow, how many kids are going to show up? Well, many days very few of the older boys missed school on those days. Most of the six, seventh, and eighth graders came. Now if we had regular classes we may not have come, but most of the time we spent those in the woods hunting and perhaps making sling shots or perhaps cutting whistles from tender popular tree branches. Oh! I wonder how many of you older folks can recall using the **red rubber inner tube strips** to make the slingshots out of.

It was unusual for us to have a lot of snow until January or maybe February so it is December and approaching the Christmas season. When we lived on Jameson Drive you may perhaps remember that we, Bob and I, put on the boxing gloves several times to settle up; which Bob always came out on top. Well, at Butler, we had a boxing team, and also many of the other school around did to. I am telling you this in order to share with the world the time that Gene Golf and I are fixing to have that, **getting together** that I said was going to happen.

It turned out there was going to be a boxing exhibition to entertain the folks at the Christmas program. So who do I draw, but you guessed it, Gene Golf. Just to make it a little easier to allow you to feel a little sorry for me, I will tell you that Gene is probably the best boxer around. Least wise, that is for the first time in my life that I had ever been knocked out cold. Now this never happened again, not that I got any better, I just never put the gloves on again.

Now in the spring we had a soft ball team that played other schools, I don't think that we ever did very well. When you play schools that had more kids in one grade then we had in the whole school it is hard to compete, however we had a lot of fun. I went to school in the seventh and the eighth grades at Butler grade school.

Let's go back to the farm living.

Other than the usual chores such as milking the cow, leading her to water every day, providing her with feed, and cleaning her stall, the cow was set for the day. That is until the evening comes, then milking starts again. Then there are the horses. They need to be watered, fed and their stalls need to be cleaned also. These chores had to get done everyday rather or not it be in the summer or winter. Now in the winter it was a great deal harder to accomplish than it was in the summertime. Mainly in the winter we had to get up, get our chores done and get ourselves ready for school. One thing that I recall is in the morning when it is real cold, if you did not have on a pair of gloves your hand can stick to the iron handle of the pump and sometimes it is rather hard to get it loose. It may be of interest to you, when we watered the animals we used a number two wash tub. If a person were to not dump out the water that night, most of the time in the wintertime it would be frozen the next morning. You'd have to break up the ice before they could drink.

Oh, I just remember a neat little thing, well it may not be so little or not as neat as I was going to project at first. But……well let me tell you what I was going to say and you can make the decision whether the incident is neat or if it can be made little of.

A while ago I mentioned the **two holer** as most of you know that I was referring to an **outside john**. Well, in the summer time you have to contend with mosquitoes and flies because there are cracks in the hastily put together outhouse. Now in the winter time there is an altogether different situation to contend with. Can you imagine when you get up in the morning and the urge to go to the bathroom hits you like a freight train and you have no time to spare? I can see it now, you jump up grab some clothes and some shoes, charge down the stairs, and then rush out the door into the dark, then squirm over to the toilet, getting in and set down just in time to prevent you know what, then you get a big shock! For the cracks in the walls had allowed the seat to be covered with about two inches of fresh snow. Oh wow!! Did that ever feel good!!

There is one thing that ought to be mentioned. Do you wonder what had happened to the corn that was obviously planted when dad got the farm? I think that it would be great to tell you how that we harvested it. It took a while to cut the stalks with a hand held sickle then we would put them in piles, well not really piles, but what we called shocks. What that consisted of was stacking them upright, several stalks then tying them together near the top. Now we did the whole field this way so when you were done there were a lot of shocks around about the field. I guess I ought to explain why that we did it this way. We had no corn crib so there was no place to store the ears of corn ,with this method of putting the stalks in shocks, we were able to get the corn out of the shocks as the corn was needed throughout the winter. The horses loved the corn.

I would like to tell a life changing experience that occurred that first fall on the farm. It would not be right to not to let you know that dad had not changed all that much, I guess that he had some sort of job I do not remember him being around the farm much accept at night. I do know that he still drank.

On this particular evening dad told us that he is going to get married. Now I am not sure if they got married before she moved in or afterwards, but either way, there she was. Now at first it was great to have a woman around so that we could have some new kind of cooking; now I am not saying that Jim couldn't cook because he was a good cook and dad was always able to drum up some good chili.

It was not long after Marie moved in, when her oldest daughter, her husband, and their three children moved in too. This created quite a house full. At first, it was not all that bad, but as time went on things started to get a little touchy, if you know what I mean.

Not in my short life time or since it got to where it was not so short, meaning now that I have grown up, it is unusual for more than one family to live together and get along as if they were one family. Now for a short period of time it may be alright but after a while some problems are apt to start showing up. I am not a family counselor. I do know this, however, that once you have some space, or even some liberties that we were used to for most of our life taken away or perhaps limited somewhat, it was not good. We were old enough to recognize what was happening. Maybe I should explain what I meant when I said what I said. I may get myself deeper and deeper into a hole, not that I may be in trouble but that you folks as the reader may be getting so confused about what I am trying to get across, I will say this…… I get confused myself.

Maybe I was a little jealous or perhaps I was feeling sorry for myself but I started to notice changes in the household mannerisms. Certain family members were allowed to be first at things. At least that is the way it seemed to be. However, the way it seemed as a child may as an adult be understandable. I guess that the trouble that we had was not really, as an adult, a big deal, but to us youngins' who felt that we had freedom now and that our so called freedom was now, in our minds, being infringed on.

I would like to share an example with you, as most of my family and friends know I am a staunch Detroit Tigers fan, even though there were very few televisions, if any. My favorite pastime was to listen to the ball game on the radio. The incident that I want to share with you took place in the summer of forty eight about the second season after they won the World Series in forty five. I was fifteen years old. You need to know that this floor model tube type radio belonged to my step mother and when it blew a tube, which it did often, I was the varmint that got blamed for the tube getting too old and give up its usability. The punishment for this crime was I was never to be allowed to use the radio again. I have never forgotten about that.

Later on, Chuck, Marie's son and his wife came to live with us. However, it was just for a short while. I suspect that the day that dad and Chuck, both of them were drinking beer at the time, and my dad weighing about 110 pounds and standing up tall at around 5 feet compared to Chuck's 6 foot frame weighing in at about 220 pounds; can you imagine what the outcome may have been, when they squared off after the beer allowed their mouth to override their brain? Yep, you are right. Dad ended up with a deep gash over his eye. I will never forget that day or even the next day either. The next day Harry, remember he is that brother who was so tough? Me and Betty and Bob were in the current patch picking currents at the time, when Harry came walking up. When he heard about the fight and how that dad got hurt he got pretty upset. Now Harry was not one to curse but when he saw Chuck up by the barn watching us, Harry called him a stupid coward. Now this really made Chuck, what we call, **red face mad**, and he took off a running after Harry. Now I would like to tell you that Harry blacked both of his eyes, But Harry probably played it smart and outran Chuck to safety.

There are a couple of things that I feel of importance, least wise to me anyway. The first thing I need to reiterate is that my step mom was a very good cook. However, being a fine cook did not really make her a good communicator. Now to get across this message I must explain, that understanding the feelings of others, is part of being a good communicator. Now I have gotten it set up so that I can tell you this story.

It all started one Sunday at our mid-day meal, Marie had prepared a mighty fine lunch. The boiled potatoes were out of this world with plenty of that white flour gravy onto them, with fried chicken. Oh so good!

Now it is time to tell the story, it goes like this. I was not really hungry, but I thought that those potatoes were so very good that I just wanted some more. By now the potatoes were all gone, so as a substitute, I ate some of the peelings that others had left on the table. I put a substantial amount on my plate with a healthy helping of that white flour gravy. All of sudden out of the shadows, a harsh cry came, **"What are you doing?"** As the startling question rang out, then there were some remarks that I did not want to hear. The final result was I no longer was not to eat someone else's left overs. Now to this day I have not and never will deprived anyone of eating until they had all that they could eat or at least all they wanted.

During the first winter that we were there, at Christmas time, dad bought me a pair of skis. Now I can just imagine that I am going to practice up for a real live shot at getting on the US Olympic team in the very near future. Well I strap on those bad boys, and take off for my first practice run, I must have been a picture of ideal form, the grace in which I handled myself on the slope must have been awesome to the eyes of the spectators, Well, I had gone about six feet when I went over a two foot drift, and much to my disappointment, both skis broke in half! Well, never did get invited to the Olympics.

I want you to imagine this, it is time to go back to school again and this year I start Ludington High school. Isn't that neat and I getting to ride the bus? This was alright and things were going along fairly good, especially since Harry was in the freshman class also. Now both of us went out for football. Harry played in almost every game but 'ole Ray, I don't think got in a game the whole year. However, I think that the experience I got in the practices helped me in the year to come.

 Then one day probably about the first of November dad proclaimed that we were packing up and were moving back to the city. This was not what I wanted to hear, I can imagine that this ole boy may have gotten pretty upset. I can also imagine that they we have had enough of this problem child so they sold the animals and left me to myself. I was fourteen years old. His was fine with me because I felt that I could make it by myself.

 Well, even though it was kind of rough, I managed to stay warm by cutting up the boards in the barn. Now it took a lot of boards to keep a fire going all night, most of the time the fire would go out. Most of the mornings I just would not start it back again. My bed was a couple of kitchen chairs right near the stove. I can imagine that there is some concern about what I could be eating in order to keep from going hungry. I will admit that the fruit that my folks had canned up from the summer crops were not all that great of a diet to provide all the nutrition's needed to sustain a healthy body over a long period of time, but it did helped.

One day after school there came a knock on the door I opened it and there stood a law officer .The message that he was bringing to me is that I could no longer stay here by myself .He asked if there was someone that I could live with. All that I could think of was my mother and Grand pa Ted. The nice police officer took me to Scotville and mother and Ted took me in.

Chapter Eleven

The opportunity to stay with Ted and mom was God sent, of course I did not really realize it because there wasn't any influence of God's kind of ways, so I had no way to sense that God was the one in <u>charge.</u> The realization of God and his influence did not occur until later in life.

Let us take a look at my new home. This was a small house that was crudely constructed. Unlike the farm house that I had come from, there was no electricity; however there was a pump on the back porch. The reason it was I there was that it was where they put a shallow well pump, what they did is take a desired length of pipe, attach a sand point to the pipe then drive it in to the ground until it is at the proper depth. It is impossible to know how deep to go for I have no idea.

Now the house is located about one mile from Scottville. You go south on the Scottville Road, go across the Peermarquette river bridge and just as you clear the river swamp you will come to two lane drive that goes to the left then down this drive about two hundred yards sets the house .

Some times my memory does not hang in there so good, there are times I have a difficult time of getting the facts straight. What I am referring to is I just don't recall who was living there at the time. I can remember Mary and it seems that Norma was there also. Carl may have already gone to fulfill his dream of going out west to become a rancher. I may be wrong but it sounds good. My place was the couch, I will say this. The couch was a whole lot better then the two hard chairs that I was sleeping on at the farm. Oh, how good it seemed to a nice lumpy couch to lie my body on. Just imagine no more meals of nothing but canned fruit. Do not get me wrong I like canned fruit but not without potatoes or something else.

Do you recall I had shared with you how that Ted was a good fellow? Now I appreciate him all the more. I had already been going to Ludington High school and dreading changing to Scottville High in the middle of the semester. Well, it turned out that I did not have to. Ted worked at Merricks salvage yard, which was located about half way between Scottville and Ludington. Now Ted was concerned about my problem and so he volunteered to take me to school in the morning before he went to work. How I got home was my responsibility. I could bum a ride, hitch hike a ride giving my thumb a job or there is the possibility of walking home. Now don't start feeling sorry for me, I have never had it so good, since the days that I did not know any better, besides when I came from football practice in Ludington several times I had to walk home from practice. This was about eleven miles.

The time went by rather quickly and soon the semester was over and it was time to start Scottville high. I guess other than the usual things that go on when you try to fit in. There was no one at the school that I knew other than a couple of guys that we, meaning my brother Leroy and, I had met.

I guess that it is a good time for me to tell you a story about how easy it is for a girl to cause a lot of trouble for two innocent people. We were at the Scottville movie theater just a watching the movie, when Mary kept messing with….. or for a better word….. flirting with a couple of boys sitting down in front of us. Now this was mo fault of Leroy's or mine.

Now I need to tell you that this incident occurred before I started school in Scottville. Those boys perhaps thought that we were intruding into their territory. So when the movie was over we went out of the theater across the street to the parking lot to leave. Mary was with us. We noticed a several fellows following us, however, when we got to the car we noticed there were more of them than we thought. A fight ensued…more like a one sided fight. When they were through with us, we got into Leroy's red convertible and left the scene with a few cuts and bruises. The weird thing about that unfortunate occurrence in my life was hard for me to forget because I knew a couple of the culprits. I Figured that I would be able to recognize them, I do not think I saw their face but one was a very big guy, not a huge fellow, but one that had obviously eaten a lot of 35cent hamburgers. The other guy I would recognize when I saw him. Now these two and perhaps others might come back into play in this chapter.

Well, I may have been able to ride the bus to school but that fact that I had been used to walking, I made the decision to walk to school. The first couple of weeks were sort of uneventful. My cousin Don was going to Scottville, high school at this time he was in the tenth grade. Now this was nice, first this gave me someone that I knew, and it gave someone to chum around with. Don was in the agriculture class the same as me. This class perhaps provided more opportunities' for a new student to get acquainted with the class such as this one. Remember the fellow I thought I'd recognize when I saw him? Yep, you got it right; there he was in the same ag class even though I don't think that he really recognized who I was.

That's what I had assumed. But as the days went on I began to reevaluate my first conclusion. What this person kept doing really irritated me…he kept calling me under classman. Now under more normal conditions I may have just ignored the comments that he was apparently making and was trying to make me feel some what of an inferior person. I had found out that this guy was failing some of his classes and was placed in the same bookkeeping class that I was in. It seemed that he needed to make up a credit, well, when he walked into the upstairs room I guess that he could not resist the chance to call me an underclassman for the last time.

Now I suppose that you wondering why the last time? Here is what happened, when he walked by, I grabbed his arm and pulled it up behind his back. I pulled it up high enough so that he was standing on his tip toes. It would be good for you to know that that back in those days there was no air conditioning, so on a warm day the windows were wide open. So with this in mind, I marched him to a open window. My intention was not to hurt him, but let him to know that this ole boy did not want to be bullied any longer. The only thing that I said to him was that if he did not stop calling me underclassman the next time I would push him on out the window, not just half way. Half way was plenty far enough for him to see the cement sidewalk two stories down. Would I push him on out the window? No, but I will say I got the message across because he and I became friends afterwards. It was all downhill the rest of the school years to come. As for the other guy, you know the one that was fat? He was in the tenth grade, I would occasionally see him in the hall ways however we did not have any problems.

Over that first year it was sort of quiet, that is after the fight situation, Cousin Don talked me into playing basketball with the F.F.A. basketball team. This team played several of the local school FFA chapters. Even though we were not that great, we did manage to win a game occasionally, this experience may have been beneficial to me down the road.

Even though the time when I tried out for a little league team and failed to make the team. I wanted to go out for the high school team. It was disappointing when they told me that I since I had transferred from another local school I would have to wait out the rest of the year.

It did not take so very long for the summer to go by. We did pick up several jobs during our summer vacation; Most of the jobs were helping farmers to harvest their crops, most of which were piece work. I think that strawberries paid ten cents a quart; sour cherries were twenty five cents for a four quart basket full. Then pickles were the big money crop, but you had to have a way to get the pickles to the graders. The grader was piece of equipment to size the pickles to the desired size, the larger pickles got one price then the smaller ones and the smallest ones got the most of all the others. Once they had graded all of the pickles that you brought in they weighed each size in and that is how that you got paid. They kept a record of each load that came in from each farmers patch. Sometimes it was very necessary to do it this way because there may be several picking groups picking the same farmers pickles.

School starts back, and the first thing, even though I did not get invited to spring practice, I went out for football, I started on the Jr. Varsity and when its season was over they took me up to the varsity squad. Now I will tell you Ray was not afraid to hit but I sure had a lot to learn.

Again I played FFA basketball and we had worlds of fun.

Now I could tell you about the regular school classes but I can imagine you are already bored with the sports part of the story. Do you recall when I said that I was not good enough to make the little league team in Ludington? Now it is time for baseball try outs. I scurried around to find a glove to use. I found one, it did not have a web attached to it, the best that I could do was to take a shoestring and make my own web. I made the team, and even then, I may not have gotten to play in a game but once or twice all year. I sort of would like, well not really like, but feel as I should confess, that the real reason that I made the team was we needed more than twelve people to field a team in case someone were to get injured. But none the less my name was on the roster.

After school was out in June a bunch of us guys got a job with Stokley brothers canning plant. Stokley's primarily featured the canning of green beans. However, they did while I was employed with them, can spinach and they also did some things with strawberries. I am not sure what else took place but I think that in the summertime when it was pickle picking time, they put the pickles [cucumbers perhaps would the proper name] in large vats then added salt and who knows what else. They put a heavy weight on top and let vats set a few months. When the proper time is up they then process the pickles. Perhaps by the time that we finished at Stokley's it was drawing near time to start getting ready for school again.

Even though my sophomore year was great, my junior year was better yet…. then of course my senior year was just awesome! I was not lacking for anything that I may have wanted or at least perhaps, I had better say, I needed. I had worked all summer and had saved some extra spending money. Believe me I liked to spend it too. One thing that Don and I enjoyed doing at noon time is rushing the three or four blocks down town to the pool room in time to get us a table. There we would stay until we just had time to run back to school and arrive just as the bell started to ring. This is an everyday occurrence during my junior year. Loads of fun!

Even football was much more exciting than ever before. Last year, I played guard. Now do not get the idea that I was ungrateful for the chance to play guard. Oh I appreciated that opportunity and I now realize that the guard position is vital to the game of football. However, all positions are of importance.

Now when I was playing the game in high school I felt that most offensive positions were really not where this ole boy wanted to play. I wanted to play defense as that's where a person could get in some heavy hitting. Now the realization that is all about contact and since contact was what I was all about, it may have made me a good guard. The reason that I came to this conclusion is that since it was offense that I was playing and my desire was to make contact and the only opportunity to do so was to be really aggressive at the guard position, I was. That is why that the guard position is where I would stay.

I have already shared with you that my junior year was a very good year and it started out with the football season. Yes, I am stuck with the guard position again. However, this is not the most exciting thing about this new season. Guess what I have been penciled in at the defensive end spot. I guess you could say that this has made my day. At least it did in 1951 it did. I sure had a lot of fun that year.

There was something that happened during my junior year, which perhaps helped me to overcome some of the shyness that has always plagued me during my school years. The Mason County school board for this year had hired a new English teacher. Now you wonder how this hiring a new teacher can be significant enough to say that it helped someone to help overcome or at least help them to be less shy. Now this new teacher was one who really communicated with her students, she was able to get me and others too, to understand the basics of the English language.   In fact, her class was a real inspiring experience for me.

Football is now over this year we won a couple of games which may seem to you, to be a not a very good team and that's the way it seemed to us too. Then came the FFA basketball season, now this was another story, we won a few games and my theory is, if you are winning it is more fun than it is if you are losing.

When spring came along it was now time for the baseball season. Now I call myself to be smart enough to realize ,since there was several new players signed up for baseball, that it may be a good idea to try out for the catchers position, not only for the security factor ,but the catchers and the pitchers started a couple of weeks before the others were allowed to start. My thought was if I were to put my face in front of the coach as much as possible that the coach was bound to get tired of seeing my face so much that he would let me play just to get me out of his sight. The coach declared that all the baseball players were expected to go out for track so whenever we got the chance to we would do a lot of running. Now the coaches got together and when there was a track meet we were excused from baseball practice. Very seldom did the two sports interfere with each other.

In track, most of the time I was assigned to run the 220 yard dash and the 220 leg of the medley relay. I really did not like running these spots because it seemed that I always was gasping for air. I recall one time at a meet we did not have anyone to run the mile. No one would volunteer and I was not concerned because everyone knew that with my speed, the coach would never pick Bigsby. There I was, with my head turned the other way, when the coach's voice broke the silence, "***Bigsby***" was the name that broke through and above all the other noise and was heard by all those around, *"you need to toe the line for the mile run."*

There was nothing else to do but to try and I gave it all that I could. I can leave it on the table and let you do your job let you think that I came in first. However, I did not, but I did finish the race. I can recall this. By the last lap, it had gotten so bad that I felt that slow motion would be exaggerating the speed in which I was moving….. not running. By the time I passed the person in front of me he was lying on the ground. So I didn't finish last….just next to last. I thought that I was going to die, well not really die, but I felt that if it were possible, I Could just lie down on the ground and stay there for couple of days I would feel much better in a couple of weeks. I got over it in a little while and life goes on.

Well a most uneventful baseball season came and went and the school is over and we are glad to get started on a new summer break.

The summer was not all that much different then the summer before, work and the recreation was much the same as last year with the exception of going roller skating nearly every night. Now we had been going occasionally during the school year. There was one thing that was exciting for me. I got a car; a 1939 Chevrolet. It was a cheap vehicle but it was mine and it seemed as though it were an expensive Cadillac.

About three weeks before it was time to start fall football practice I was following cousin Don, he had gotten a big Packard car. We were going down this gravel road when he brought his mighty Packard to a stop. Well, this was unfortunate because by the time that I realized that Don had stopped and I was, I admit, traveling too close, going too fast for the conditions, and was not paying close enough attention to what was going on; my poor car looked as if it had plowed into the rear of a big Packard car. My car was demolished; Dons car had no damage whatsoever. It was kind of hard to own up to my carelessness, however my fear that Ted would be big time upset over the accident was unfounded because after a show of disappointment everything was fine in fact he knew where he could find another car. The second car that I had was a 1939 Chrysler which I kept until I went into the Army.

My senior year……. "Wow", this without a doubt will be the greatest year of my teenage years.

For one thing they put me as line backer on the football team; this is where they should have had me all along. Remember, I had shared with you that offense was not my favorite spot to get stuck on. Always before they had put me at offensive guard; not this year I have been assigned to the quarter back position. Now if I wanted to I could ride a glory train just because of the title of the position. If you recall the last couple of years, my job on the team was offensive guard, and I had expressed that the only way that I could get the satisfaction of contact was to be real aggressive. I guess the coaches saw this so they decide to put me in as the quarterback.

Now I would feel less guilty if you were knowledgeable about the offensive formation that we were using. First thing, the quarterback did nothing other than call out signals, block for the running backs, and occasionally go out on a pass pattern which was designed to deter the defensive backs away from the intended receiver. Everything was going fine this football season. That is until during one game when I did not ran the pattern that I was supposed to run. What is meant by that is, instead of going the route I was supposed to I got a little too deep and much to my surprise the half back threw a perfect pass, what a feeling it was to make a touchdown. At the moment I felt that this hero had saved the game, however it felt to me it was not necessarily received as a great play by the one that was supposed to have gotten the pass. However, when he was sharing his thoughts about the play, I can imagine that I must have not scored a touchdown, but I must of ran the wrong way and scored some points for the other team. However that is his opinion but not mine, I scored a touchdown!!!!!

Now before I go on with the rest of the football year I need to bring you up to date regarding brother Bob and brother Harry. Harry has transferred from Ludington High for the purpose of being at the same school as two of his brothers. There is no doubt that if he had been eligible to play in Ludington he probably would have stayed where he was. It seems that his age, which was 20, put him above the legal age of eligibility to play in any participating games. Bob, who had been going to Scottville and was a tenth grader this year, played football too. Do you recall when we lived on Jameson Drive? How Bob was so much quicker than I was? Well, Bob was still quick in fact Bob made the varsity team as a freshman. Well Hurry's desire was to be the manager of the football team so he could be around the field when we were playing, He got the job and it was great to have him there. I guess that it would be good to the reader's ears if I were to say that we won the state football championship in our class that year, but no, we did not win the state but we did win some games that year.

Here is a little bit of information that you may be interested in, three brothers going to the same school and living in three separate places. Bob had taken up with a farmer He got room and board to stay there and work on the farm. Harry was still with Grandpa Bigsby, and I of coarse was still with Ted and my mom, it really was a fun time for the three of us.

I would guess that by now you might think that sports might be the only thing that we were interested in. Now as time goes on, there are other things that are beginning to interest this shy country boy. Perhaps being elected the president of the FFA, and not wanting to make a fool of myself, I felt as if I ought to give the job my every effort, and I did. However most people would have done a better job with less effort, but we survived the year. At least until it was the end of the year FFA banquet. At the end of the president's speech, that I in my mind, said something of this nature,

"Now for the faculty I hope that there will still be some necks and feet left", it was fairly obvious that chicken was the main course. I am not sure how the faculty took this blunder but the boys sure liked it. I was embarrassed somewhat but I was a senior and knew that I would be out of there in a few days.

There was another subject that I found a liking for and that was English. Now this did not rank as high as sports, however, I had a choice to take or to not take English in my last year. I do not know how it is today but in Michigan in the fifties if you did not make at least a c grade you were required to take English class during your senior year. I liked the subject so well that I decided to take English my final year. I just assume that some of you are thinking that ole Ray did not make a passing grade; well I would like to inform you that taking English was of my own choosing.

This new teacher that came last year helped me a whole lot. This is one of those thoughts that just popped up in my mind. This teacher was so influential to me and where I was headed in life. It is ironic that during my life I have always found a certain attraction to red hair, now I know why, the English teacher had red hair. BINGO.

While we are on the English class and the red haired teacher, and believe me I do not understand why, I got an A for playing a small part in the senior class play. No not for a lead part, but a very small but important part in the play. I was sort of glad that spot was mine it was not that hard even though I still made a booboo. Instead of saying "Indian" I said "injun". It was a western type play. We made it through the play.

There is one occasion that I would like to bring up. It reminded me of it just now because what happened during the play. It seems that it was getting closer to production time and there were only a few more practices left. Some of the actors were having some difficulty with their parts; by the way this included me. Her request was that the final three practices would be mandatory. There were three or four of us that had jobs, but even though this may cut down on my spending money, I could sense the need, to miss work and to be at practice. I realized that when I was setting pins at the bowling alley, if someone were not to show up I would just set double and make more money, no problem. The play was important and I didn't want to hurt the teacher's feelings or be embarrassed.

With football over with and FFA basketball completed, we are now starting the last semester and as a senior this meant easy times. There is one thing that I would like to share with you. When basket ball season was over it was always a tradition to have the annual senior/faculty basketball game. Now since there were not five seniors on the varsity team they asked a couple of us other seniors too play. I know that they knew that I played on the FFA team. Now I brought this up for a specific reason even though it is not the time to share that reason I will tell you what happened. It was not because I was a great player that I scored 18 points, high scorer in the game, I will come back to this.

The 1952 baseball team was no better than any other year but it was not any worse either. I did get to play more this year, not too good with the bat but at least I was about average with the glove. I think if there was such a person, the baseball gods were starting to look after this struggling baseball player. Any way the last game of the season, the seniors get to play the whole game; there were three or four spectators in the **standing room only** home side of the field. If a person had not brought a chair, since there was no bleachers...... so a crowd this large had no where to go either...... stand or stand.

I can imagine the humongous ovation that took place when this slugger stepped o the plate. (NOT) Just think with a .ooo batting average the score keeper may have already penciled in the score book beside my name just as he had the previous time that I had come to bat. However, much to everyone's amazement and to mine also; when the pitch came, I guess that I closed my eyes as usual, and with a mighty swing, somehow the ball went whizzing over the head of the third baseman! I was so shocked when I ended up on second base. Much the same look on the coaches face and I gather that he was rather surprised as well as I was.

I am not sure that you realize the impact that this might have on my baseball career. My very first hit in three years of high school baseball, wow, was I ever excited. That was worth all those **slivers from riding the pine** for all those games. It soon became my turn to come to the plate for another time at bat, now at this time I probably thought that it might be better if they would let someone pinch hit in my place. That was not the game plan, I took my turn as scheduled and much too everyone's surprise I hit another double to left field. This ended the season and I can say that I was very happy.

Now the year is about to come to an end. The only thing left was the sports award night. Now I could tell you that I was a hero and received many awards but this was not so. The coaches went through the list until the very last. Then he announces a new category for an award, the new award was to go to the person who was a good sport in all of the sporting programs in the school, football, FFA basketball, track, regular basketball, and baseball. I was spellbound by receiving that award.

After the sports banquet was the senior skip day. Of course this was an unauthorized event, and there were warnings given to discourage this annual defiance of the principal's rules. However, we went on with the plans anyhow. There was only one minor incident that slowed us down. One of the cars, carrying the seniors to Lake Michigan had a flat tire. Several of the boys manually picked the car up and held it up while others changed the tire. After the tire was changed, we went on our merry way to a day of fun. Now we knew that we must get back to school in time for the folks that ride the bus. Well, we got there in time to catch the bus but guess what? The principal declared an early release from school so no bus. The only thing left for us that had wheels to transport us home was cars so there were lots of people that needed rides to their homes, All in all, this was worth every inconvenience that we had to put up with.

Now the only thing left is my very first date in High school. This occurred at the end of my senior year. I mustard up enough nerve to ask a person whom was as shy as I was, to go with me to the senior prom. This girl, a bright young lady, was as nice and polite as anyone else in the senior class. Now I treated her with the respect that she deserved. I was too shy to treat her anyway else. Anyway I got her home at an early hour safe and sound. This was my very first real date and I can say this it was nice. Thank you Fluorine Shoup. If you read Mom's Garden, you will find out about the kiss.......

Now that school is out it is time to prepare for my life later on. I got what I thought to be very good job with continental motors in Muskegon, a town about 55 miles to the south of Scottville. In the meantime, I had started a correspondence course in TV and radio repair. I had a nice job at the continental. For a while I commuted to work, and then later I got a one room apartment and came home just for the weekend. This worked out very well, that is until in April of 53 Uncle Sam pointed his finger at me and said I was needed to help save the world. From that time forward for two years I was his.

Chapter Twelve

For a nineteen year old who had learned what it was about being on his own, with plenty of throw away money, and a car to ride in. I reported to my employer about my being drafted and they assured me as long as they could, they would keep my employment open when I return and that sounded good to me.

Let us take a look at some of the other boys' dealings with the military. Leon, the oldest, had recently gotten out of the Navy. Milbert who had enlisted into the Army was now at Louisville, Kentucky. Harry enlisted into Army airborne and now is in Fort Bragg, North Carolina. Bob enlisted in to the army and was now in South Korea. The rest of the clan is accounted for too. Dwayne was living in Michigan, my sister Betty was married and living in Michigan and Leroy was still living with Pa but was now married to Mary.

Now that you have been caught up with there is one small thing that I would like explain. That 39 Chrysler that I had which was not allowed to go with me on the airplane, it was my choice to give it to Leon so he would have a car to use.

I reported to Jackson, Michigan and there I was sworn in., Can you imagine the U S of A depending on one shy backward country boy being part of the force to bring us to victory. There is one thing that happened during my physical, now do not be embarrassed when I tell you, I was embarrassed enough for all of us. Can you imagine, there I was standing for what it seems to have been five minuets, buck naked, They wanted me to move my trigger finger, they wanted that crippled finger that got mashed way back on Jameson Drive to work. Well, they figured that I ought to be able to fire a gun. Anyway, the next day they loaded us on a plane headed for El Paso, Texas. My first airplane ride was in a raggedy old D C 3; I will assure you that this was not a luxury liner. We ought not to complain, we got there in one piece. They then loaded us up in buses and took us to Fort Bliss. Ft. Bliss is located in the far west corner of Texas close to the mountains and in the desert joining the white sands of New Mexico.

They gather us all up in a large assembly hall to give us our assignments. Now I had heard several times, do not volunteer for anything. With this in mind, I decided to keep my yap shut. Now the person at the podium asked a question, now I recognized that was just asking questions not seeking volunteers. The question went something like this. ***"Is there anyone here that has any cooking experience?"*** Promptly, I held up my hand at that time and realized that I had done what I had been warned not to do. However, it turned out fine. The experience that I got that month in the mess hall helping the cooks was great. About the third day, I was in the mess hall the mess sergeant asked me to make some lemonade. Now even though it was April the heat was sort of hot in the day but it got cold at night. Anyway I knew I could drum up some mighty tasty lemonade. A long as I was there my biggest responsibility was to keep lemonade in the refrigerator. One day however the mess sergeant assigned me to make a pot of spaghetti. Now I knew how to make spaghetti so I jumped at this responsibility. Always before a rather small pot is what I had used to do the job. This time the pot we were to use was a ten gallon container. I am thinking that the main difference is more boiling water and more spaghetti .What a huge mistake after we put the pasta in to the water, the water was no longer boiling and the noodles came out in big chunks, we had to throw that batch away and try again.

Well, my thirty day wonder as a cook was now over; I would like to let you know that it was not a mistake. I learned a lot about basic training. There was a time that really gave me a huge lift, this was when a call for me to report to the battery commander's office .Now in my mind ran all sorts of thoughts about what did I do wrong? Well, when I reported to the commander he told me that I had a visitor. Well, there stood my brother Bob who at this time was a sergeant who was going home on leave. We had a nice visit then he was gone. Well basic training wasn't as bad as I had drummed it up to being. It was not long and it was over. Most of the time was spent on 60 millimeter anti aircraft guns. There were some stuff like marching and night maneuvers', and rifle range, and gas chamber, and early revelries, and close order drills, and, calisthenics', and another night march, and I suppose all of this was good, at least I feel as if this ole boy was a better person for the things that we went through. THANK YOU Uncle Sam.

It was quite a leave from basic training and the time off while I was waiting until it was time to report to Fort Hamilton, New York. It was a good time to be had because both Bob and Harry were on leave at the same time, what a surprise.

After the time off, I Got to Fort Hamilton just in time to find out that I was being sent to an isolated antiaircraft site on the outskirts of a New Jersey town. I am not really sure if this is proper or not ,but I assume since 55 years has passed and revealing that location by now may not be considered an act of bad boy stuff. Anyway this antiaircraft site with its 60 MM guns which we trained on was upgraded to 90 MM guns. Also, the outdoor tracking apparatus had been upgraded to an indoor satellite with a large screen. Now in 1953 there was a great concern that by air we needed to keep an eye on our Eastern sky. Now I was here at the New Jersey site until the summer of fifty four, it was at this time that I was promoted to Corporal and transferred to Sandy Hook. There were only a few of us there, the work load was unbelievable. We were so far away from any military activity we were the only contact with anyone with the exception when we were off duty.

I was very fortunate to have met a family in New Jersey who took me in and allowed me to stay in their upstairs apartment. There were three bedrooms so it worked out very nice for me. In fact, while I was at Sandy Hook, I hid my foot locker and things that I really did not use in an old ammo bunker. I needed a way to get from Elizabeth to Sandy Hook. So I purchased a 1940 Pontiac coop. A very nice ride and I kept it until I got my papers to go home. It was not a very exciting military tour of duty if it had not been for the first month and the last week while I was preparing to go home, It may not any different than anyone else's army duty. After saying that it I suppose I ought to share what happened that last week.

It started like this, on the last day we were called to a mustering out formation; this is where we were to get our separations papers. It was perhaps around 1300 hours. That is one o'clock real time. There was a question asked, after you look at your seperation paper and if there is any mistakes raise your hand. Do you recall when I first started basic training I mentioned that I was warned not to volunteer? The biggest problem that I had was not that there was a mistake on my paper. My problem was what happened next.

Well I did it again, when I was asked "What is the problem?" I shared with the sergeant that my serial number was not correct. Thinking that this was vital for my freedom I did as he instructed .However not paying any attention and seeing the things around me I opened the Warrant officer's door. I stepped up to his desk and went to give him my papers so they could be corrected. The Warrant officer looked at me with a very stern glare and asked, "***Soldier can you not read?***" I could tell by the smile that was nonexistent on his face that he was about to make a point. I had a very strong feeling that the point that he was about to make was not going to be in my favor. He took the paper from my hand and replied, "***What do you need?***" When I told him that my serial number was wrong, then after he had looked the papers over, he put the papers on the corner of his desk. The time at this point was about 15 hundred hours. He replied that I had to wait and since I had to wait anyway it would be a real good thing for me to wash the windows for Uncle Sam.

As unhappy as I was I felt that might be better if the windows were better off if they were all broken out. Of course I came to my senses and got a bucket of water and a rag and started washing the windows as it was suggested. Remember it was 15 hundred hours when I brought the papers in to the clerk's office. Now I sort of watched the clock and the papers out of the corner of my eyes, fifteen minutes passed by the clock moved but the papers were still on the desk in the same spot as they were earlier. As the time was going by I began to become very concerned that if I were not to get to the pay roll department on time that means that it would not open again until Monday. As the time past I kept watching that paper that was still sitting on the desk in the same spot. I can just imagine that Warrant Officer was really enjoying this which is okay but I would much rather it was someone else.

At 1645 hundred hours a secretary picked up the papers, corrected the number then called my name. She instructed me to look it over to make sure there were no other discrepancies. I did notice that my name was misspelled, at this time of the day I was not going to turn loose of these papers again until I was safely out of the army missed spelled name or not. I was now a free man and all that there was for me to do is get to grand central station then on to Michigan. I took the ferry to the mainland then went to catch a subway to Manhattan then to Grand Central. To make this worst day of my life more affirming to be the worst day, I had to wait about fifteen minutes for the next subway. Well I went into this small diner to wait a few minutes. It came time to catch the subway so I did. When we had gotten across the Manhattan Bridge, where is my duffle bag? Oh no I left it at the diner. I got off the subway went across the station, caught a subway going back over the bridge. Things were starting to look a little better for it was no big deal to get my duffle bag then I headed across the bridge on to the station.

I gathered up my belongings something was missing, oh no my AWOL bag was not there. After a thought or two I realized that I must have left it when I changed subways at the bridge. Well, I hurried back to that stop only to my disappointment I did not see it anywhere. A nice fellow I assume to be a janitor asked what was I looking for when I told him he pointed to a wooden box and explained that he had put it in the box incase the owner came looking for it. I told him thank you and went on my merry way. That was a very rough day.

Now that the military obligations are complete, my job with Continental was no longer available I chose to do a little traveling. So a friend of mine set our sites toward California.

Now if you think that you might like to know what took place later, pick up the book ***Mom's Garden.***

Mom's Garden

Prelude to wet your whistle- You have to encourage him to complete the garden.

(Unedited version…..)

As you recall I had promised to write my recollection of what took place between the time that I finished the book Oops Pops leading up to the time to start the book MOM'S GARDEN . If you recall I shared the inkling that a friend and I had planned to purchase a pair of motorcycles and go on a joy ride out west to California .According to my memory the events that took place during those days, some fifty some years prior to this day may have not been necessarily true, but again it's what I recall not necessarily what happened.

It may be of some interest to you all how this came about. After I had gotten out of the Army and the job at the Continental was no longer available. I proceeded to find work elsewhere. My dad lived in the Flint area. The message got back to me that they were hiring in the automobile industry. The first place that I applied for a job was at Fisher body. Fisher body is a plant where the parts for such cars as Chevrolet, Cadillac, Olds, and other GM products were assembled. I will never forget my job it was my responsibility to put the body parts onto a traveling conveyer. Each automobile required different body parts, it would have been great if they would have put together all the same vehicle at one time then changed over to a different model until they had the required quota of each one. However, this was not the plan the whole system was to put the car together as the orders came in for whatever one was next in line. I would have suggested the other way but since I was new on the job and since my job allowed no time for extra thinking I figured that in the next minute there would be another body part to put on the conveyer. This went on over and over each car requiring about five parts. During this peered while my stay in the Flint area I was staying with my brother and his wife Maggie this was at the time when Jamie was a baby. I recall lifting him over my head and since the joy that he had by the way he would laugh uncontrollably, what joy he brought to my life. It is about this time that Don Ruthruff contacted me with the idea to get a pair of motorcycles and do some traveling, it seemed to me aver good plan. When I went to work at Fisher body I had purchased a 52ford Don had a 1950 ford so we decided to sell his car in the spring and start our trip in the newer car .First one thing then another happened and by the time we were to leave it was already midsummer nineteen fifty five. At first we were to travel to Florida to visit his folks in Florida. Our plan was to pick up odd jobs along the way then go further and when our cash run low then we start to look for another job. There were three different places that we stopped to work from the middle of July to the latter part of October. The first was in Livonia, Michigan, the next was in MAUMIE Ohio as was the third. The job in Lavonia was at a boiler plant, it was an all right job, it paid well for the year 1954 however two dollars an hour was not enough to change our plans about our trip, so after a few weeks we moved on to Maumie, this was a very interesting employment I would like to share with you about sour Kraut and how it was made. I recall back on the farm we made Kraut by putting shopped cabbage into a five gallon crock adding salt to it than putting a weight on it then it stayed like this until it was ready to make the Kraut, perhaps it may have taken several weeks. Primarily this was the same technique that was being done at the Kraut plant with the exception instead of a five gallon crock the one they used was about twenty feet high and it had a diameter of about eighteen feet. I will say this that size of a vat will hold a lot of chopped cabbage. Now the weight that they put on top of the cabbage was made of three layers of two by twelve's one layer running one way the next layer angled then the last layer cross the other way again. Perhaps the point that I wanted to bring out was the method of getting the cabbage out of the large vat. Everything is not real clear so what I tell you may be somewhat fabricated, but it may be close to the truth. It seems that there was a platform around the top of the tank, after the weight was removed then it was our job to clear the contaminated cabbage off the top which consisted of about six-inch to around a foot of bad cabbage .Once this was accomplished we started to dig out the good cabbage, put it into containers, each container held around four ton of wet cabbage. I will never forget how people would react when we would tell them that we loaded forty ton of Kraut in one day. This particular job only lasted for about a week. Next we went to a local farmer whom we were told needed some help to help harvest the apples. This farmer was great I can never recall any one setting up two containers of apple cider, one regular cider and one container with hard cider. This stuff was really good in hot weather. Now it was time to move on to Florida to visit Don's folks before going on to hunting gold so that we could get rich.

Least known to me there was gold in Florida too, in the form of a red headed beauty right in my path…….

And a garden grew……… just a few…..tune in soon!

Pops